Folk Music and Dances of Ireland

D1394144

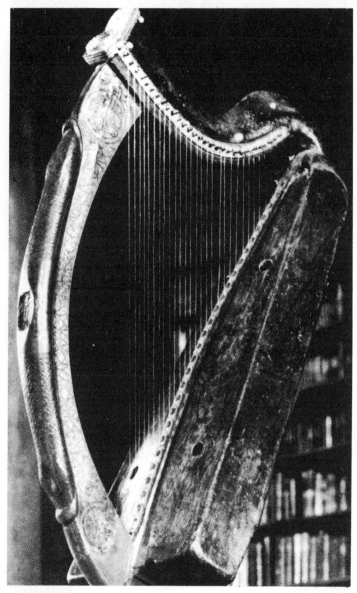

FIGURE I. The 'Brian Boru' harp; fourteenth century.

Folk Music
and Dances of
Ireland

A comprehensive study examining
the basic elements of
Irish Folk Music and Dance Traditions

Breandán Breathnach

O S S I A N

Music Copyist: Dennis Suttil
Design by John Loesberg
Printed by Colour Books, Dublin

The musical examples in this book are available
on CD (OSSCD3) and may be ordered from your
local music/book/record shop or directly from
the publishers.

N.B. The list of selected recordings on page 143
dates back to Breandán's original selection for the
1971 edition. Updating this list would have been a
possibility, but given the subjectivity of any
inclusion the publishers have preferred to leave
things as they are.

Ossian Publications
P.O.Box 84, Cork, Ireland
ossian@iol.ie
www.ossian.ie

OMB 123   ISBN 1 900428 65

Contents

D'aos oirfididh Éireann

Foreword

This short account of the folk music and dances of Ireland is offered as an introduction to the subject. It derives from an acquaintance with this music at first hand over many years, from knowledge gained in discussion with other practitioners, and from research and reading. Footnotes and references to sources, in a general work of this kind, would lead to overcrowding and on that account they have been avoided, except in the case of direct quotations. However, readers consulting the books recommended for further reading will find for themselves much additional information on points which could be only briefly treated in the text.

Associated with this work is a recording of genuine traditional music performed in an authentic manner. Readers, then, not familiar with this kind of music may, if they wish, hear it for themselves. Readers wishing to reproduce the sound will find the detailed transcriptions of this music in Appendix I of help.

I am most grateful to the performers who played and sang this music for me, to Pádraig Ó Máille for transcribing the song airs and for other valued assistance, and to Tom Munnelly for letting me use his recording of John Reilly's singing. I am indebted to The Director, The Irish Folklore Commission, for permission to use *Laoi na Mná Móire* and to the staff and the correspondents of the Commission for much help and unfailing attention. My grateful thanks are due to Dr T. Wall for bringing to my notice some rare sources of information. I hope a general word of thanks will be acceptable to the musicians and others who supplied information or set me right on points of detail. All faults and shortcomings I freely acknowledge as my own.

Breandán Breathnach

1. Irish Folk Music

Bím lá binn agus lá searbh.
CEATHARNACH UÍ DHÓNAILL

I

FOLK-SONGS have been described as the songs of the people. If one were to make a collection of the songs of the Irish people, one would hardly hesitate about including *The Last Rose of Summer* and *Silent, Oh Moyle* from Moore's *Irish Melodies*, patriotic songs like *My Dark Rosaleen*, *The Memory of the Dead*, and *Boolevogue*, and some of the songs of Percy French. If the collection were to be restricted to folk-song, however, all these would have to be discarded, since however national, however popular, they may be, they cannot be regarded as folk-songs. The term 'songs of the people', then, is too wide for our purpose, and an equivalent in Irish, *amhráin atá i mbéal an phobail*, also embraces too much. (In fact, this term nowadays might be a better description of pop music than of folk music.)

What makes these terms unacceptable is that they include songs which, though they may express the sentiments of the people, are the work of known writers and on that account must be ruled out. This suggests that folk music and song are the product of the folk and, accordingly, anonymous, and it is in this sense that the term 'folk music' is used in this handbook.

Songs, however, do not write themselves, nor is music composed by 'the folk'. Folk music, like all other music, is in the first instance the work of some one person, but since it is accepted by—and becomes the property of—the community, and since it is passed on from generation to generation, so that it no longer possesses any features which would link it with a particular school or class of writers or composers, we speak of it as anonymous. Folk music is a heritage which is passed on from one age to the next—hence the term 'traditional', which is usually applied to it in Ireland. Irish folk music includes not only the older songs and melodies of the Gael, which are undoubtedly our most precious heritage, but also the Anglo-Irish and English ballads of the countryside and the extraordinarily rich vein of dance music which belongs exclusively neither to Gaeltacht nor Galltacht.

II

Only a few isolated pieces of the great body of Irish traditional music can be regarded as purely instrumental, in the sense of music played solely to delight the ear and not for dancing or marching. In olden times the contrary was the case, as many references in the ancient literature attest, and that the three thirds, *suantraí, geantraí* and *goltraí*, into which music was divided refer only to instrumental music is evident from the ancient legends which purport to explain the origin of these terms. In the account of the battle of *Magh Tuireadh* fought between the Tuatha dé Danann and the piratical Fomorians it is related how the Dagda (the good god) effects the release of Uaithne, his harper, who has been carried off by the retreating pirates. He pursues the fleeing band to their retreat,

FIGURE 2. Seated figure playing harp. A plaque on the reliquary of Moedoc (Mogue), the earliest example of this theme in metal; eleventh century.

where he sees his harp hanging from a wall on which they have placed it, and the harp comes to him at his bidding, killing in its passage nine of the pirates. The Dagda plays upon the harp the three musical feats which give distinction to the harper. He plays the *goltraí* until their women weep; he plays the *geantraí* until their women and youths burst into laughter; and he plays the *suantraí* until the entire host falls asleep.

Another legend relates how the three sons of Uaithne were named from the music played on the harp while *Boand* (the river Boyne, a goddess), their mother, was in labour:

> The harp was crying and mourning with her at first in the intensity of her pains—it was laughing and making welcome with her in the middle at having brought forth two sons, and it was a soothing and sleep-inducing strain it played with her on the birth of the last son after the weight of her labour: it was from it that a third of the music was named.

Elsewhere the names are derived from the music played on a harp of three strings. An iron string named *suantairghléas* produced music which threw all who heard it in a deep slumber; a brass string called *geantairghléas* gave music which made all the company merry; while the music of the third string, one of silver, the *goltairghléas*, plunged all the company in deep sorrow.

The division of the music into the thirds was little more than a literary convention, one, indeed, which continued in use over a thousand years while the native literature maintained its vigour. The various explanations for the origin of their names, however, were highly imaginative attempts at explaining the origin of the music itself or its introduction into Ireland, and it is fanciful to regard the terms as indicating a technical classification of the music.

FIGURE 3. *(opposite)* Piper. A panel on the Cross of the Scriptures at Clonmacnoise; tenth century.

Commissioners of Public Works

5

One is on surer ground when considering the musical instruments in use in ancient Ireland, since actual objects and not literary conventions are now in question. The references already quoted from the old legends show that the *cruit* or harp enjoyed pride of place. In fact its music was the only kind that ennobled a person in its own right. Frequently associated with the *cruit* was the *timpán*, which from its name one might suppose to be a tambourine or percussion instrument. (The Latin *tympanum* signifies a drum or tambourine.) The Irish *timpán* was, in fact, a stringed instrument which was sounded with a bow. The performer on the *timpán* is mentioned in the ancient poem describing the Fair of Carman which is found in the *Book of Leinster*, a manuscript written about 1160. Fiddles, *fidle*, are also mentioned in this poem, but while the term in all probability refers to a stringed instrument played with a bow, it was not, of course, the modern violin, which was developed in its present form in Italy only in the second half of the sixteenth century.

There was a profusion of wind instruments in use, but the descriptions available do not permit precise identification. The *buinne* was probably a horn-shaped trumpet, the *corn* a long curved metal one, and both are more likely to have been instruments of war and of the chase rather than musical instruments proper. The *cuiseach* probably represents the earliest type of musical instrument, one made of stalks of corn and reeds from which the pith had been extruded. The *cuisle cheoil*, musical pipe, as the name indicates, was a pipe or tube of narrow bore. It was probably made of cane or hollowed wood and sounded by having a tongue or slit cut in it to form a single reed. This instrument may well represent a development which occurred when the method of boring had been discovered. The *feadán*, referred to in an old story as *foghurbhinn* (sweet-sounding) was a whistle. There is no reason to believe that the *píopaí* or pipes referred to in the ancient tales were not a type of bagpipes. Reference in the laws and elsewhere to *pípearadha* (pipers), and *cuisleannaigh* (pipe blowers) indicate a clear distinction between these performers and accordingly between the instruments played by them. *Cuisle* is a native word, *píopaí* a loan word. If the assumption is valid that the word *píopaí* has retained its original meaning, it is safe to infer that the *cuisle cheoil* was a musical pipe, of the kind, for example, being played by the angel on the Cross of the Scriptures (Fig. 3), and that the *píopaí* or bagpipes was not an indigenous or native instrument in Ireland. It remains to add that the *píobaire* and *cuisleannach* belonged to what were legally regarded in ancient Ireland as inferior professions.

2. The Structure of the Music

Even in their liveliest strains we find some melancholy note intrude—some minor third or flat seventh—which throws its shade as it passes, and makes even mirth interesting.

—THOMAS MOORE TO STEVENSON
(February, 1807)

I

PEOPLE coming from art music to Irish or other folk music are often surprised to find that many airs do not close on the expected key note or its triad but seemingly are ended on other notes of the scale. To those with a knowledge of church music this is not a novel situation; it is merely further confirmation that there are other kinds of music than those encompassed in the two divisions of major and minor melodies into which western art music falls. Irish traditional or folk music, it will be found, may end on any one of four particular notes, and by reference to these the music may be divided into four classes. It should be stressed that by the ending or final note is not simply meant the last note of an air as it would appear in a transcribed version, but the final note of rest or repose on which the melody can be fittingly brought to a close—to the ear of the traditional player, however, and not necessarily that of the art musician.

In the great majority of airs the final note is, in fact, the last note of the air. This is almost always so in the case of songs and marches. In the case of dance music, single and double jigs and hornpipes most commonly end on this note, but a great number of reels and an even greater number, relatively, of the slip or hop jigs

8

end on a note designed, not to close the tune, but to lead into another strain or into the start of the tune itself. Such tunes because of this feature are known as circular tunes. All, of course, can be made to end on the appropriate final note and are so ended when a player concludes a bout of music on playing one of them.

The four notes on which Irish traditional music ends are, to give them their solfa names, Doh, Ray, Soh, and Lah. Since the airs and tunes in heptatonic or seven-note scales predominate, and as more than half of these end on Doh, the related scale will be adopted to illustrate the system into which this music fits:

FIGURE 4. First Scale, Doh. The scale of C major is chosen here because it permits the system to be illustrated on the white notes of the piano.

A new scale can be formed from these eight notes by a process called *inversion*, that is, by detaching the lowest note and placing it at the top of the series. Continuing this process so that each note in turn becomes the basic or starting note, we end up with seven distinct scales, including the first with which we started. We stop at seven, of course, because the series begins to repeat itself at the eight note or octave. Of these scales or modes Irish folk music makes use of four: the first C to C¹; the second D to D¹; the fifth G to G¹; and the sixth A to A¹. These series are most conveniently called by their solfa names Doh, Ray, Soh, and Lah, although this method of naming them is liable to mis-interpretation. It is not to be inferred that the relationship between the notes of a scale implicit in their solfa names exists likewise between these scales. Each exists in its own right and possesses its own tonic or fundamental note.

9

It will be noticed that the first or Doh mode (the Ionian of church music) is composed of seven intervals which correspond to those of the ordinary major mode of art or studied music. The fifth or Soh mode (the mixolydian of church music) also corresponds, except at the seventh position. The second or Ray mode (the Dorian of church music) differs in two positions, the third and the seventh, while the sixth or Lah mode (the Aeolian of church music) corresponds to the harmonic minor mode of art music except at the seventh position. The relationship of these scales to each other and their points of difference are more clearly illustrated by setting them to end on the same final note.

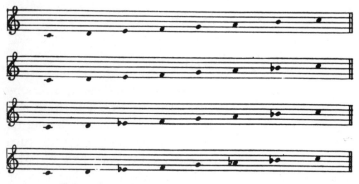

FIGURE 5. Taken from the top these are the first (Doh), the fifth (Soh), the second (Ray), and the sixth (Lah) scales written to end on the same final. The differences in these scales are pinpointed by the 'flat' symbol (♭).

It has been mentioned that the first or Doh mode is the predominant one in Irish folk music. In fact over 60 per cent of our music belongs to this mode. Among the airs and tunes in it are *Eibhlín a Rún*, *Éamonn a' Chnoic*, and *Róisín Dubh*. Examples occurring in the text are *Cailín ó Chois tSiúire mé* (page 19), *Dunphy's Hornpipe* (page 140), and *Concertina Hornpipe* (page 141). Pieces ending on Soh account for approximately 15 per

FIGURE 6. First (Doh) scales in the heptatonic, hexatonic, and pentatonic series. Non-occurrence of notes is indicated by the symbol X.

cent of the total, and include such airs as *Spailpín a Rún*, *Bánchnoic Éireann Óighe*, *The Blackbird*, and *Hardiman the Fiddler* (page 135). Airs in the Ray mode, accounting for somewhat over 10 per cent of the music, include *Eanach Dhúin*, *The Boyne Water*, *Cailín Deas Crúite na mBó*, *Elizabeth Kelly's Delight* (page 136), and *The Congress Reel* (page 133). Airs in the Lah mode are the least numerous. Examples of airs in this mode are *Thugamar féin an Samhradh Linn*, *An Cóisire*, *Bruach na Carraige Báine*, *The Dear Irish Boy*, and *My Love Nell*. A mixture of modes in tunes occurs very occasionally, usually taking the form of the first part being in Soh, the turn or second part in Doh.

It is of interest to note that English folk music, by and large, falls into these same four divisions and the proportion of airs in each division is surprisingly close to the Irish figures.

The scales or modes referred to above have been described as heptatonic, that is, having seven notes within the span of the octave. Two other systems of scales are of importance in Irish music. These scales are the pentatonic, having five notes to the octave, and the hexatonic, having six notes to the octave. If we treat these two systems as we have treated the heptatonic scale, it will be found that the whole is in correspondence, except where the gaps or spaces occur in the lesser scales. The first pentatonic scale corresponds with the Doh mode, except that it lacks a fourth and seventh. The first hexatonic corresponds except that it lacks a seventh.

One hears from time to time, admittedly in rather vague terms, that pentatonic melodies are a marked feature of Gaelic (Irish and Scots) music. An examination of the Irish material, however, does not confirm these assertions, as such melodies constitute only a relatively small proportion of the national repertory.

II

The scales used above to illustrate the system into which Irish music fits were chosen for convenience in layout. The underlying principles may be applied to all airs irrespective of the pitch or scale in which they are played.

As the tunes and airs played by traditional musicians are almost without exception played in one or two sharps, the application of these principles to the instrumental music as performed by these players can be demonstrated in quite a simple manner.

Tunes with ♯ ending on	Mode or scale	Tunes with ♯♯ ending on
G	Doh	D
A	Ray	E
D	Soh	A
E	Lah	B

It will be noticed that the ending notes D, A, and E in this table are common to both series. A problem arises in allocating to its class a tune ending on one of these notes if 'C' is missing from it. If 'C' does not occur in a tune which ends on D, one cannot say whether the tune belongs to Soh in the first series or to Doh in the second series. The case is similar with the other two pairs. In the absence of 'C', a tune ending on A may be regarded as either the Ray of G or the Soh of D, and a tune ending on E as the Lah of G or the Ray of D. The distinction between the two groups is that 'C' is natural in the first and sharp in the second. As will be seen later the note must be strong or in an accented position to play this role.

It will be noticed that no reference has been made to accidental notes in the scheme above. In fact, two such notes occur. They are C♯ and F♮. C♯ occurs usually by way of variation and almost invariably in a weak or unaccented position. For example, the triplet

may replace and may be used in

place of where both d's are accented. These

remarks apply to the note as it occurs in tunes of the 'G' series. In tunes of the 'D' series, C is always sharp, whether in a strong or weak position.

F natural, on the other hand, occurs only in the accented position. Its occurrence is somewhat of a mystery. It does not occur very frequently and it cannot be used at will, merely as a form of ornamentation. It is more often found in the upper than the lower octave, and its presence seems to be confined to tunes in the 'G' series. It is one of the highly colourful notes of Irish music, and is made by sliding upwards, with a certain amount of vibrato, from E to F sharp. It is a note, therefore, of no fixed pitch but rather a long glide with a centre somewhat sharper than the F natural of art music. On that account it cannot be sounded on an instrument with fixed notes (e.g. the piano), or a keyed flute, and when it occurs in a tune it is better to play F sharp instead on such instruments.

C natural, likewise, is a highly decorative note, possessing several colours on the pipes which are exploited to the full by the skilful performer. It lies approximately half way between B and D, and by definition can occur only in tunes belonging to the first or G series of our scheme. It is of interest to note that it is these two notes, C and F, which are lacking in the pentatonic scale, and their mobile character may derive from this fact. The fact that tunes making use of these two colourful notes are found only in the G series may be an indication that such tunes belong to an older tradition than most of our dance music.

Broadly speaking, it may be said that the other intervals correspond to those used in art music. Piano and accordion, radio and gramophone, have had a levelling effect over the years on the scales and intervals of the music.

III

The vast majority of airs have a range varying from nine to eleven notes. Scarcely any exceed a range of thirteen notes, and few have less than an octave. One freak, *Harvey Duff*, has only two notes, at least in one Dublin version. It was whistled, from a safe distance, after policemen by groups of children on the streets of Dublin sixty or seventy years ago, being repated *ad lib* or until the policeman was provoked into giving chase.

Har-vey Duff don't take me, take the fel-low be-hind the tree.

By and large, song airs and dance tunes consist of two parts or strains, each containing two phrases of equal length. Unlike dance tunes, which always have at least two parts, there are a few song airs which have only one strain or part. Distinguishing the phrases as A, B, and so on, we may note the various ways in which the phrases are combined, e.g., A A A B, A A B A, A B B A, A B C D .The most common form is A A B A (the sonata form) and one on which many of our greatest songs are modelled. Among them may be mentioned *Éamonn a' Chnoic*, *Seán Ó Duibhir a' Ghleanna*, *The Derry Air*, *The Little Red Lark*. Airs formed on the pattern A B B A include *Jimmy mo Mhíle Stór*, *Fáinne Geal an Lae*, *Róisín Dubh*, and *Our Wedding Day*. Airs on other models, e.g., A A A B, A B A B, A B C D are rare. In dance music the basic form may be expressed as A A¹ B B¹ where the repeated phrase is modified to conclude the strain or provide a run in to the following part. Where a part is played twice or doubled, the pattern may become (A A¹)2, B B B A¹. The form A A B C is not infrequent in reels, while some hornpipes disclose their origin in song airs by the form A A B A.

3. Song-Airs and Songs

Perhaps we may look no further than the last disgraceful century for the origin of most of those wild and melancholy strains, which were at once the offspring and solace of grief.
—THOMAS MOORE in *Irish Melodies* (No. 3)

I

REFERENCES to the playing of music are frequent in our manuscript literature, but since no system of musical notation was used in olden times in Ireland, no specimens of the music played are available. Bunting's description of airs, 'Very Ancient, Author and Date Unknown', sheds no light on the age of our music; and in the absence of dated tunes, it is not possible to examine a body of music and assign types with certainty to particular periods. It would be rash to declare that because Irish music may be described as non-harmonic, it belongs to an age before harmony began to be developed. Some airs and tunes may indeed be pre-seventeenth century, but labelling them as such is largely conjecture.

Political and social changes affect the national repertory. The change over from Irish to English throughout the greater part of the country, proceeding apace for the last two centuries, has been accompanied by a major loss of music and songs. The popularity of the patriotic songs in vogue after 1916 resulted in older

FIGURE 7. (opposite) *Callino*; from a sixteenth-century manuscript. *By permission of the Board of Trinity College, Dublin*

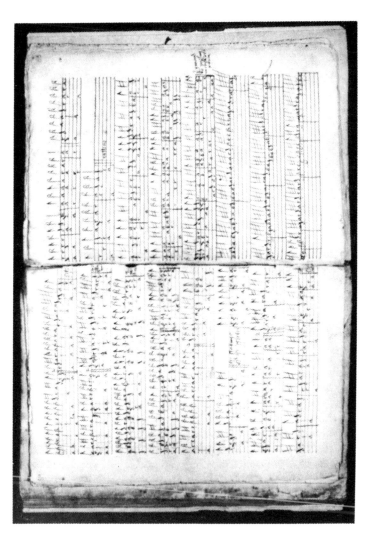

17

local songs being forgotten in some rural areas, whilst the replacing of one type of dancing by another using a different time inevitably led to the disappearance of many dance tunes.

While the tradition is still living, the national store maintains itself, later additions offsetting losses of older material. As might be expected, the result of this process is that the later rather than the earlier predominates. Most of the airs and tunes preserved in the national stock were, in all probability, composed in the last three centuries, the greater number most likely belonging to the latter half of the eighteenth century and the opening decades of the nineteenth. There may be older elements in the national repertory, sustained like particles of matter in a stream, but until the extant material has been indexed, classified, and analysed one may only speculate about the age and origin of our music.

One Irish air can with certainty be assigned to an earlier period. The jumble "callen o custure me' in Shakespeare's *Henry V* (IV 4) has been deciphered to read *Cailín ó Chois tSiúre mé* (I am a girl from the Suir-side). In a poem beginning *Mealltar bean le beagán téad* (a woman is wooed with a few strings) found in a late seventeenth-century manuscript from Fermanagh, *Cailín ó Chois tSiúre* is mentioned with the names of other songs, the singing of which, the poet declares, would have been a more profitable occupation for him than writing poetry. Malone, the great Irish eighteenth-century editor of Shakespeare, in his effort to restore the correct reading, has drawn attention to the appearance in *A Handfull of Pleasant Delites*, published in 1584, of a song entitled 'A Sonet of a lover in the praise of his lady, to *Calen o custure me*, sung at every line's end'. The air is found among a collection of songs and other pieces bound together with William Ballet's

FIGURE 8. *Callino*; in modern notation by P. H. Corran.

lute book (belonging to the last quarter of the sixteenth century) now preserved in the Library of Trinity College, Dublin. It is the earliest known annotation of an Irish song and will be immediately recognised as a variant of that to which *The Croppy Boy* ('Good men and true in this house who dwell') is sung.

The first text we find associated with an air is that of *Is brónach mo thocht*, a lament written by the Kerry poet Seafraidh Ó Donnchadha, who lived in the second half of the seventeenth century. The occasion of the poem was the death of the poet's spaniel Druimín, which was choked when a mouse being chased by a cat jumped into its mouth. The song has no less than twenty-seven verses, and it is directed to be sung to *Iom bó agus Um bó*, a refrain with which each of the verses is ended. There are several songs bearing this name. One set by Petrie and described by him as a dirge (Stanford's Petrie no. 1202) fits the words without any straining or stretching, so that it is safe to conclude that it is the air to which the song was intended to be sung.

Down to the middle of the seventeenth century the poetry of literature was composed in syllabic verse, that is, in metres which were based on the number and arrangement of the syllables in the line and stanza. Poems composed in this form were not intended merely for silent reading, but also 'to be agreeable and pleasing to the Ear', and the full savour of their intricate sound patterns was brought out by the *reacaire*, whose function it was to chant them at feasts and assemblies presided over by the chief. A most interesting description of this performance is found in a work published in 1722:

> the *Action* and *Pronunciation* of the Poem, in Presence of the *Maecenas*, or the principal Person it related to, was perform'd with a great deal of Ceremony, in a Consort of Vocal and Instrumental Musick. The poet himself said nothing, but directed and took care that every body else did his Part right. The Bards having first had the Composition from him, got it well by Heart, and now pronounc'd it orderly, keeping even Pace with a Harp, touch'd upon that Occasion; no other musical Instrument being allow'd of for the said Purpose than this alone, as being Masculin, much sweeter, and fuller than any other.

What airs were used by the *reacaire* on these occasions we shall never know, since it was not the practice at the time to commit music to writing. It was thought that since the metres employed in bardic verse derived from those used in the Latin hymns of the early Church, the chants employed had a like origin. They may indeed but not for the reason stated. It has now been established that these metres were in use long before the introduction of the Christian hymnology into Ireland.

FIGURE 9. Reacaire: from Derricke's *Image of Irelande;* sixteenth century.

It was not until the destruction of the bardic schools in the middle of the seventeenth century that the metres emerged in which all our songs are composed, although it is certain that these *amhrán* or song metres had been cultivated for a long time before that. Unfortunately, compositions in these song metres were beneath the notice of the *file* or professional poet, and on that account found no place in the *duanaire* or official anthology.

As in the folk music of other lands, love songs constitute the most numerous class of folk-song in Ireland. Unmistakably deriving from the popular poetry of the Middle Ages, the themes and types prevailing are a legacy of the Norman invaders. Their adoption into Irish is believed to have begun towards the end of the thirteenth century.

All moods and feelings are reflected in these songs, from the simple delight of the uncomplicated courtship to the numbed resignation following separation. Songs expressing grief at the loss of a lover or the bitter realisation of betrayal (e.g. *Úna Bhán, Saileog Ruadh, Dónall Óg*) attain an intensity of feeling and passionate sincerity that are irresistibly moving. The stressed vowel pattern on which the songs are formed and the freedom of the music from adherence to a rigid tempo, blend, particularly in songs of the kind mentioned, in a perfect union of liquid melody.

The symbols and metaphors in use, although drawn from the common environment, are richly poetical and imaginative:

(1) Is áille í ná grian an Fhómhair,
    's go bhfásann mil ina diaidh
    Ar lorg a cos sa sliabh,
    Dhá fhuaire an uair th'éis na Samhna.

(2) Nach aoibhinn don chábán a dtéann mo ghrá-sa
    ag ól ann?
    Nach aoibhinn don chasán a leagann sé a bhróig
    ann?
    Nach aoibhinn don chailín óg deas a gheobhas é
    le pósadh?
    Réalt eolais na maidne agus crann soilse an
    tráthnóna.

(3) 's gur milse blas a póg ná siúcra beach ar bord
    's a bheith ghá ól ar bhrannda craorac.

Patriotic or national songs of a folk character are remarkably scarce in Irish. One such song, *Róisín Dubh*, which immediately springs to mind, was elevated into that category only in the last century. It is a love song and, despite assertions in tourist literature, almost certainly had nothing to do with Aodh Rua Ó Dónaill. The emotional need for this type of song was met, perhaps, by the *aisling* or vision poetry which enjoyed a tremendous vogue in the eighteenth century, especially in Munster.

The *aisling* was a literary, not a folk creation, but since the associated airs were traditional, a brief description of this type of poetry will not be out of place. In a dream or vision, the poet, wandering alone, spies a *spéirbhean*—literally a skywoman—coming towards him. He describes her appearance, being particularly lavish in his description of her hair. When they meet he questions her as to her identity, mentioning the names of all the ladies he can recall from Irish and classical mythology. She is none of these, but tells him at last that she is Ireland, grieving under the oppression of foreigners who shortly shall be driven from the land.

The *aisling* type and other patriotic songs written by the eighteenth-century poets were composed for oral circulation, not for silent reading. They were wedded to airs already well-known, and so were immediately available to the whole community. There can be little doubt that these literary pieces ousted, to some extent, the purely 'folk' song in Munster. On the other hand, the high artistry displayed in many of the folk-songs must owe something to the fact that the literary works of the trained poet did circulate orally within the community.

The designation of Ireland by names such as *An tSeanbhean Bhocht, An Druimíonn Donn Dílis* or personal names such as *Caitlín Ní Uallacháin* or *Cáit Ní Dhuibhir* was a favourite poetic device in the eighteenth century. It is stretching things too far, however, to see in it the expression, by way of allegory, of political discontent which could not be openly expressed in plain verse. The device is so patent and the general intent of the songs so plain that one can hardly believe it likely that state officials or local justices could have been taken in by it.

Many of those who study the poems of Fionn and the Fianna as part of the school curriculum fail to realise that these are ballads—stories set in poetic form intended for singing at assemblies. These *laoithe* form part of the *Fianaíocht*, the last great cycle of the native literature, which began to take its modern shape in the first half of the twelfth century. Fionn, the fair one, originally a figure in mythology, had by then been found a place in the pseudo-history of ancient Ireland as captain of the professional soldiery maintained by King Cormac Mac Airt, who lived in the third century. The exploits and adventures of Fionn and his band of warriors are recounted as being told to St. Patrick (in the fifth century) by Oisín and Caoilte, who had survived all the other members of the Fianna.

Here again we are indebted to the *Book of Leinster*, which contains examples of the new balladry that have been assigned by scholars to the opening decades of the twelfth century. It is tempting to see in this fresh use of an older native form a development prompted by the west-European ballad but as scholars place the emergence of that balladry a century or so later, one must look to the surge of literary activity which marked twelfth century Ireland for the origin of the Fenian lay.

The Fenian lay was usually set in stanzas or four-line verses, each line generally having seven syllables. The themes are wholly romantic and magical—encounters with otherworld beings, the slaying of monsters, elopements and pursuits, invasions, and overseas expeditions. Over the centuries the lays were tremendously popular with all classes of Gaelic society, from the most southerly tip of Ireland to the most northerly point of Gaelic Scotland. Possessing a high poetical quality, they can still delight, although the chants to which they were performed have been lost in Ireland.

O'Curry affords us an evocative glimpse of the world in which they had their being:

> I have heard my father sing these Ossianic poems, and remember distinctly the air and manner of their singing; and I have heard that there was, about the time that I was born, and of course beyond my recollection, a man named Anthony O'Brien, a schoolmaster, who spent much of his time in my father's house, and who was the best singer of Oisin's poems that his contemporaries had ever heard. He had a rich and powerful voice, and often, on a calm summer day, he used to go with a party into a boat on the Lower Shannon, at my native place, where the river is eight miles wide, and having rowed to the middle of the river, they used to lie on their oars there to uncork their whiskey jar and make themselves happy, on which occasions Anthony O'Brien was always prepared to sing his choicest pieces, among which were no greater favourites than Oisín's poems. So powerful was the singer's voice that it often reached the shores at either side of the boat in Clare and Kerry, and often called the labouring men and women from the neighbouring fields at both sides down to the water's edge to enjoy the strains of such music (and such performance of it) as I fear is not often in these days to be heard even on the favoured banks of the soft flowing queen of Irish rivers.
> o'curry, *Manners and Customs* (Vol. iii, p. 392) (1873).

O'Curry speaks of the lay as being in his day on the verge of extinction. Actually it survived into the present century, and collectors of the Irish Folklore Commission recorded two sung versions of *Laoi na Mná Móire* from two old men in the Glencolmcille district in Donegal over twenty years ago. It is as a judgment that their

25

names, Mícheál and Séamas Ó hIghne, are here recorded as the last two people in Ireland to sing an Ossianic lay, for with them perished a tradition which extended back almost a thousand years. That manner of singing now survives only among the oldest inhabitants of the Hebrides. Happily, Scottish scholars have recorded several of these pieces from the living tradition.

Mícheál Ó hIghne's rendering of the *laoi*, the most interesting musically of the two, is yet pitiably corrupt in text and music. Because of the interest it must hold for readers familiar with the *Laoithe Flannaíochta* a composite version of the air, deriving from several stanzas, is transcribed hereunder. The chant-like

Do bhí Sceolán agus Bran ar éill
ag Fionn réidh ina dhóid,
Do bhí a chú ag gach duine den Fhéin,
Is ár ngadhair bhinn bhéal ag déanamh ceoil.

FIGURE 10. A composite version of *Laoi na Mná Móire* devised by Pádraig Ó Máille from phrases as sung by informant but not in the order in which he sang them. The verse of the *Laoi* derives from another source. The original recording was used by kind permission of the Director, Irish Folklore Commission.

quality and free rhythm style, reminiscent of Latin plainchant, may be observed in the music.

The lays recorded in Scotland share in these features and there the opinion has been expressed that these airs resemble those to which the *reacaire* chanted the bardic verse, and that like the metres of that verse they find their origin in the Latin hymns of the Church.

With the extraordinary vigour displayed by the Fenian cycle of balladry it was not surprising that the ballad themes favoured in England and elsewhere in Europe should scarcely find a foothold in Ireland. Not more than a dozen have been noted here, among which are the widely spread *Lord Randal (Cá raibh tú ó mhaidin, a dhearthdirín ó)* and the *Cherry Tree Carol (Trí scóir a bhí Seosamh nuair phós sé Muire Mháthair)*.

III

Labour or occupational songs, with rhythms to match the physical actions to which they were the accompaniment, are not common in Ireland. This is remarkable when we compare our music to the related music of Gaelic Scotland, and remind ourselves that the social conditions of the two communities in the seventeenth and eighteenth centuries were much alike. Scots music abounds in labour songs. It is particularly rich in waulking songs, i.e., those sung while the home-woven tweed was being shrunk. The process, known as waulking or fulling, was, naturally, performed in Ireland, but evidently no songs were composed to relieve the tedium of it. Another type of occupational song, the boat song, which was frequent in Scotland, is not represented here at all.

We are then singularly poor in labour songs. In fact, we should be hard pressed to muster more than a score or so. Some spinning songs such as *Maileo léró, is ím bó néró* more or less complete the count. It cannot be that such songs were once plentiful, but, like the ploughman's whistle, passed out of memory when the crafts with which they were associated became obsolete. Hand spinning and weaving, for example, survived well into the present century in Gaeltacht districts, but no songs survived with them.

Although there are some beautiful examples of the lullaby, this is another type of song which is not very well represented in the national store. There are historical reasons why religious songs are scarce, as these develop and are sustained in corporate acts of worship, and regular religious services were almost impossible for lengthy periods of our history because of the operation of the Penal Laws. As for the carols, in the modern sense of songs about some aspect of the Nativity, we can scarcely claim half a dozen.

IV

The change-over from the Irish to the English language did not occur overnight, and in what may be called the halfway stage, when a great many people were bilingual, a type of song arose in which both languages were used. Technically known as *macaronic*, these songs were composed with phrases, lines, or couplets alternating in Irish and English. They were generally of a humorous nature, most often in the form of a boy-courts-girl dialogue:

> I am a young fellow that ran out of lands and
> means.
> *Seanamhná 'n bhaile ná tiúrfadh dom bean ná spré.*
> I placed my affections on one that had gold and
> store
> *Is do gheallas don ainnir go leanfainn léi féin go deo.*

Occasionally the verses alternated. In songs made in

this fashion, the English verse was generally a translation, sometimes a close one, of the preceding Irish verse. Another common form of this type is one in which the laudatory sentiments expressed in the English verse are ridiculed in the Irish to reveal the true feelings of the singer and his audience.

It is not surprising that during this period songwriters familiar with both languages should display some features of Irish versification in their English verses. Assonance or 'vowel-riming' was a favourite, perhaps an unconscious, borrowing:

> When I heard the news, I was much confused.
> I myself excused when I thus did say
> Is O'Connell gone, old Erin's son,
> The brightest orb that e'er stood the day?
>
> *Erin's King* (a lament for Dan O'Connell)

There is a folk version in English of *An Draighneán Donn*, as well as versions of *Connla*, *Jimmy mo mhíle stór*, and *Bean Dubh an Ghleanna*. Examples of this kind of borrowing are so rare in relation to the body of Irish song that one may deduce a rule that folk-songs do not pass from one language to another.

Dancing and its associated music survived the changeover from Irish to English. Here, the music was independent of the language, and, in any event, similar forms of dancing were in vogue in the English-speaking community. The decline of the language involved the rejection of the body of folk-song which had its existence in it. Strangely enough, the associated airs were also discarded almost *in toto*. Fragments of songs in Irish and features associated with Irish systems of versification scarcely survived the first generation of speakers adopting the dominant culture, as all incentives in the community—social, economic, and political—operated against their retention.

Folk-songs in the English language fall broadly into two groups: (i) English and Scots songs, and (ii) Anglo-Irish songs. Those of the first and older group were introduced into Ireland by the English and Scots settlers of the seventeenth century and by the Irish workers who travelled to and from England during the last two centuries. Many, too, derived from the imported ballad sheets, printed in England, which circulated in Dublin and other east coast towns. In this way, songs such as *Barbara Allen, Lord Baker* (page 130), *Edward*, and *Captain Wedderburn's Courtship* were absorbed into the national stock. On such fare, for example, was Goldsmith reared in his youth in Longford. "The music of the finest singer", he wrote, "is dissonance to what I felt when an old dairymaid sung me into tears with 'Johnny Armstrong's Last Good-night' or 'The Cruelty of Barbara Allen' ". By a strange quirk of history, when traditional singing has almost passed from the English countryside, versions of songs regarded as classics of English folk-song may be recovered in satisfactory texts in Ireland.

By Anglo-Irish folk-song we mean folk-songs, within our definition, which were composed by Irishmen whose mother language was now English. The vacuum left by the displacement of Irish was filled by Moore's melodies, by stage Irish effusions, and by concert and drawingroom pieces whose only claim to being Irish lay in the use of Irish placenames and a sprinkling of 'mavourneens' 'acushlas' and such terms of endearment. The genuine English and Scots folk-song already imported, were immediately available, and the business of creating new folk-songs did not cease because Irish was being discarded, although the quality and texture of the songs altered out of all recognition.

The writers of *The Nation*, the Young Ireland

newspaper established in 1842, aimed at initiating a new era in Irish ballad poetry. Although *The Times* described their compositions as far more dangerous than the speeches of Daniel O'Connell, only some few of them achieved a permanent place among the national or popular songs. The rude simplicity of the songs composed 'by peasants of little education for peasants of still less', as one contributor to *The Nation* scornfully described the rural folk-songs, proved more acceptable and enduring than the literary artifice of the Young Ireland writers.

In the new folk-song, as in the old, love songs naturally predominated. Abductions and elopements, happy encounters and cruel separations, jiltings and jesting, provide themes covering all aspects of courtship, whilst shipwrecks and drowning disasters, murders and executions, topical events at local and even international level, all were recorded in verse. The years 1798 and 1803, the Tithe War, and every other political or national movement had its crop of song. Indeed the common muse appeared to fail only when politics became dominated by parliamentary parties!

VI

One may deduce a rule, as has already been suggested, that there is an innate relationship between folk-song and language which inhibits adoption by way of translation. On the other hand, national barriers or language seem to offer no obstacle to the interchange of tunes, especially between neighbouring countries. Borrowings of this kind have led to strange results in Ireland. *The Wearing of the Green, Viva La,* and the *Seanbhean Bhocht,* highly patriotic songs in the English language, are associated with Scots airs.

Borrowed tunes figure prominently in the stock of airs to which the Munster poets of the eighteenth century penned their verses. *Seán Buí*, the Scots *Over the Water to Charlie*, which is still played as a jig, was a particular favourite, and at least fifteen songs were written to it. Five songs at least were composed for singing to *Ar Éirinn ní Neosainn Cé Hí*, the Scots *Tweedside*, an air said to have been composed by the ill-fated Rizzio, secretary to Mary Queen of Scots. Other borrowed airs to which songs in Irish were written are *The British Grenadiers*, disguised under the Irish title *Leaba Chlúimh is Chórdaí*, *The White Cockade*, *Hielan Laddie*, and *The Cuckoo's Nest*. This last, called in Irish *An Spealadóir*, is a variant of an early Elizabethan ribald song entitled *Come ashore Jolly Tar and your trousers on*. *The Boyne Water* to which Piaras Mac Gearailt composed *Rosc Catha na Mumhan* belonged to the Scots. At the other end of the scale, the music used for children's games in Dublin and other urban areas is almost without exception English in origin.

In addition to these borrowings the Munster poets also used the great native airs to carry their songs. Donncha Rua wrote his *Bán-Chnoic Éirinn Óighe* to the haunting air *Uileacan Dubh Ó* (the Napoleonic ballad *The Green Linnet* is sung to a variant of this air); and the no less magnificent *Seán Ó Duibhir an Ghleanna* was used by Eoghan Rua Ó Súilleabháin for his *Sláinte Rí Searlas*. Folk airs are associated, then, with two types of song in Irish: the literary productions of the poets, and the impersonal folk-song. The literary songs appear to have been written to suit airs already existing; the facts do not support the opinion that the airs were composed for the words. No air has been associated with any poet so as to suggest that the words and air of any particular song were the composition of the one person.

What has been said about songs in Irish is generally true of national songs in English. There are exceptions here, however; *Boolevogue* by P. J. McCall, was originally associated with the air *Father Murphy* and is now sung to the air *Eochaill*, and both of these airs are traditional. On the other hand, the music for Ingram's *The Memory of the Dead* was composed by William Elliot Hudson, brother of Henry, the music collector, of whom some account is given at page 114.

As already suggested, music falling outside the two great divisions of song airs and dance tunes forms only a very small part of the national repertory. Of that music, marches constitute the biggest class. They are more numerous than would appear at first sight since it is certain that some double jigs were originally marching tunes. *O'Sullivan's March* and *Máirseáil Alasdruim*, both of which may be ascribed to the second half of the seventeenth century, if not to an earlier period, may still be heard played as jigs by traditional musicians in Munster.

Purely instrumental music is represented by a mere handful of tunes called 'pieces', all of which are derived from double or single jigs. These pieces were devised simply by filling in intervals in the original tunes with elaborate runs and embellishments. They were played rather deliberately, somewhat at waltz tempo, for which dance, in fact, they could quite easily be adapted. Settings of these pieces are quite commonly met with in the Munster manuscripts of a century or more ago. They are usually associated with the parent tune, the one described as 'the jigg way', the other as 'the piece way'. Pipers played some long descriptive pieces, the most well known being *Máirseáil Alasdruim* which commemorated the battle fought at Cnoc na nDos in 1647, and *The Battle of Aughrim*, commemorating the defeat of the Jacobite forces in 1691. In these pieces, the assembly of the troops and the march into battle, the noise and frenzy of the fight, and the cries of the women lamenting over the slain were imitated.

In another of these pieces, *Fiach an Mhada Rua* or *The Fox Chase*, the sounds of the hounds, horns, and horses are imitated.

Formerly traditional musicians when playing slow airs adopted an ornate florid style that rendered the airs unvocal. Petrie, as we shall see later, complained bitterly about the barbarous licence these players indulged in. Nowadays traditional musicians seldom play slow airs. They usually confine themselves to dance music and then almost wholly to playing reels. What slow airs are played are usually derived at first or second hand from printed sources. Very few have been learnt traditionally or are played in a traditional manner.

The compositions of Carolan and other harpers have been ignored here since by definition they cannot be regarded as folk music and since, with one or two exceptions, they are known only through printed texts.

It is tempting to fit airs and tunes into the old divisions of *goltraí*, *suantraí*, and *geantraí*. Laments may be described as sad music and on that account classed as *goltraí*; lullabies, with their characteristic reiterated phrases, may readily be identified as *suantraí*; and dance music, of course, would represent gay or happy music. As already suggested, however, such classification would be wholly fanciful. These three terms in Irish denoted the magical effects which the *cruitire* of the ancient sagas could produce with his music, and purely magical they were. There is no inherent quality in the vast bulk of the song airs which would indicate whether the intended effect was happiness, drowsiness, or sadness. A change in tempo can effect a change in mood, and songs of widely different sentiment have been associated with the same air. As for dance tunes, a high quality of the traditional musician is his ability to draw 'a fine lonesome reel' out of his instrument.

4. Dancing

B'fhearr liom ná spré go mbeadh rinnce agam,
is dá mbeadh, ní phósfainn ach píobaire.

I

THE lack of specific references to dancing in our older literature has led some people to suppose that dancing was unknown in ancient Ireland. In the biblical story of Salome dancing before Herod, for instance, three terms—*cleasaíocht, léimneach,* and *opaireacht*—are used in the Irish translation where the Latin text would have had one, *saltare,* and this has been taken as proof that dancing was unknown here in olden times—as if the absence of a term for the activity indicated the absence of the activity itself. A more likely explanation is that the Irish translator used words like 'acrobatics', 'tumbling', and 'activity' ('hopping' has also been suggested) to describe a kind of dance which would not have been familiar to his readers. The practice among British and continental Celts, too, of religious and pre-battle dances is well attested, and the absence of such dances among people in Ireland sharing a similar culture would be remarkable. It would be strange, moreover, if a people with a native taste for music, as is evidenced by the many different musical instruments they possessed, had no knowledge of the kindred art of dancing, which may indeed have preceded that of music.

35

In the modern language we find that the two words in use for dancing (*damhsa* and *rince*) are loan words. *Damhsa* is derived from the French *danse* or its English equivalent *dance*, and the earliest use of the word in the written language dates only from around 1520. *Rince* is a borrowing of the English *rink*, meaning to skate on ice, and it is used in that sense in Ó Cianáin's *Flight of the Earls* (1609), where it is also, however, used in its present-day sense. To add to our problem, *coir* and *poirt*, nowadays used for reels and jigs, do not properly signify these dances but quick, lively pieces on the harp. *Port* also signified an exercise in harp playing, and when a dance tune was intended the term used was *port rince*. In the spoken language *port* now means an air to which there are no words, as distinct from *amhrán*, verses sung to music. *Jigeannaí* and *ríleanna* are obvious borrowings from the English. The first derives from the Italian *giga*, an old dance which got its name from or perhaps gave its name to the *giga* or early fiddle. Reel is derived from *rulla* (Anglo-Saxon), meaning to whirl. A Scandinavian origin has been suggested for *reel*, but as the rapid movements of the dance would be most uncharacteristic of Scandinavian dancing a Celtic origin is more likely.

The Normans are given the credit of having introduced round dances into Ireland. In the twelfth century, the term *carol* indicated a lovesong dance, and it was only some centuries later that it acquired its present meaning in English. Originally associated with May day rites and observances, the carol had become a favourite pastime of the French nobility, and about the time of the Norman invasion of Ireland it was particularly popular in Normandy. There need be little doubt, then, that it was practised also in the Norman towns and strongholds in Ireland. At this time the carol consisted of a verse sung by a chanter or leader, and a refrain sung by the rest of the group, who danced round with simple steps in a ring, following the leader.

A very common form of the carol consisted of a verse and chorus of four lines, the verse comprising a line repeated three times and a concluding fourth line. This form may be represented by the formula $(3A+B)+C$. An example of this form of versification is:

Is trua gan peata'n mhaoir agam,
Is trua gan peata'n mhaoir agam,
Is trua gan peata'n mhaoir agam,
's na caoire beaga bána.

Is ó goirm, goirm thú;
Grá mo chroí gan cheilg thú.
Is ó goirm, goirm thú,
's tú peata beag do mháthar.

The first three lines of verse and chorus have four accents. The concluding lines have each three accents. When they are sung, the final syllable of the verse and chorus attract a beat. Musically, the words are borne by two strains, each consisting of four bars in 2/4 time, a measure which suits quite well many of the present-day dances. In fact, the air associated with this song is played in Co. Clare for the plain set, the strains being doubled to suit the dance. The transcription in page 139 shows that the chorus preceded the verse, a not unusual feature in this type of song. One can quite easily envisage the carol being performed to a tune such as this with its strong but simple rhythm.

The Irish 'Hey', to which references are frequent in Anglo-Irish and English writings from the sixteenth century onwards, derives its name, not from the 'hi' of the carol but from the French *haie*, a hedge. As the performance of this dance was usually described as 'trotting the hey' it is probable that it was identical with the Irish Trot, a dance to which references are also found, e.g. 'Some pace the Whip, some trot the Hay'.

From written accounts it would appear that the hey was a round dance in which men and women took part and which included figures in which the women wound in and about their partners. In Scotland the term *hey* survived into the eighteenth century, when it began to give ground to the word *reel*. The hey, therefore, may well represent an intermediate stage in the evolution of some of our present-day round dances.

Pacing the Whip, *Trotting the Hey*, and *Skipping of Gort*, which were dances of the Pale, seem tame affairs in comparison with the dances mentioned in an Irish poem of around 1670: *rince an ghadaraigh* (the withie dance) *rince an chlaidhimh* (the sword dance), *rince treasach re malartaibh ceolta* (a dance of ranks with change of music), and *rince fada re racaireacht ógbhan* (the long dance with the sporting of young maidens). Dances like these, which were traditional Irish forms of entertainment, suggest that more exciting amusements were to be found outside the Pale than in it.

II

Allusions to country dances are abundant during the seventeenth century, but unfortunately there are no descriptions extant which would enable us to guess what form these dances took. *Raingce timcheall teinte* is mentioned in a poem of the late sixteenth century, and Fynes Moryson, secretary to Lord Mountjoy, writing about 1600 declared that the Irish

> delight much in dancing, using no arts of slow measures or lofty galliards, but only country dances, whereof they have some pleasant to behold, as Balrudery, and the Whip of Dunboyne,

and they dance about a fire commonly in the midst of a room holding withes in their hands, and by certain strains drawing one another into the fire; and also the matachine dance, with naked swords, which they make to meet in divers comely postures. And this I have seen them often dance before the Lord Deputy in the houses of Irish lords; and it seemed to me a dangerous sport to see so many naked swords so near the Lord Deputy and chief commanders of the army in the hands of the Irish Kerne, who had either lately been or were not unlike to prove rebels.

> FALKINER, *Illustrations of Irish History and Topography*, London, 1904.

It seems that some of the country dances then in vogue in Ireland had been superseded by French dances in England, and had wholly passed out of memory in that country. Spenser in his *View of Ireland* (1596) refers to the old manner of dancing among the Irish as owing its origin to the original inhabitants, then believed to have come from Scythia on the shores of the Black Sea. In fact, country dancing spread from England into Ireland.

A most interesting reference to music and dancing is found in a description by an English traveller, Thomas Dineley, of a journey he made through Ireland in 1681:

> They (the Irish) are at this day much addicted (on holidayes, after the bagpipe, Irish harpe, or Jews harpe) to dance after their countrey fashion, (that is) the long dance one after another of all conditions master, mrs, servants.

Apart from the implied note of surprise that all, irrespective of station, joined in the fun, Dineley's remarks are of value because of their mentioning the musical instruments then commonly in use. The long dance in question is of course the *rince fada*. A dance of a different kind is mentioned around the same time by another English traveller, Dunton, as being popular at wakes. 'Sometimes they followed one another in a ring (as they say fairies do) in a rude dance to the musique of a bagpipe'.

Dineley's reference to dancing at wakes is also worth repeating, no less for the mention it makes of the musicians involved as for the list it gives of the Christian names then in vogue:

> At these meetings the young frye, viz. Darby, Teige, Morogh, Leeam, Rinett, Allsoon, Norah, Shevaune, More, Kathleene, Ishabeal, Noulla, Maygrett, Timisheen, Shennyed, &c., appeare as gay as may be, with their holyday apparrell, and with piper, harper, or fidler revell and dance the night throughout, make love and matches.

In a contemporary account of King James's march to Dublin (1689) we learn that,

> all along the road the country came to meet his majesty . . . orations of welcome being made unto him at the entrance of each considerable town and the young rural maids weaving dances before him as he travelled.

A later account (*c.* 1780) described King James as being welcomed on his arrival on the sea-shore at Kinsale with the *rinnceadh fada*, the figure and execution of which delighted him exceedingly. The dance, we are told, was performed by three persons moving abreast, each of whom held the end of a white handkerchief. These advanced to slow music, and were followed by the rest of the dancers in pairs, each of which held a white handkerchief between them. The music suddenly changing to a quick measure, the dancers passed with a quick step under the handkerchief of the leaders, wheeled around in semi-circles and executed a variety of lively figures before falling back into their original positions, whereupon, presumably, the marching was repeated.

The *rince fada*, therefore, in its combination of dancing and marching was somewhat like the present-day *Bridge of Athlone*. It was performed in Limerick on May eve, particularly by the butchers, and up to the latter half of the eighteenth century, when it was ousted by the new French dances, it was customary to dance it at the conclusion of private and public balls.

The cake dance, to which references are frequent in the eighteenth and nineteenth centuries, was not a particular dance but rather a *báire* or session of dancing at which a cake was offered to the couple who proved themselves the best performers. Sponsored usually by the local alehouse keeper, such gatherings were sometimes associated with hurling or other athletic contests. A delightful description of the custom was reported from Westmeath in 1682:

> On the patron-day in most parishes, as also on the feasts of Easter and Whit-suntide, the more ordinary sort of people meet near the ale-house in the afternoon, on some convenient spot of ground and dance for the cake; here to be sure the piper fails not of diligent attendance; The cake to be danced for is provided at the charge of the ale-wife, and is advanced on a board on the top of a pike about ten foot high; this board is round, and from it riseth a kind of a garland, beset and tied round with meadow flowers, if it be early in the summer, if later, the garland has the addition of apples set round on pegs fastened unto it; the whole number of dancers begin all at once in a large ring, a man and a woman, and dance round about the bush, so is this garland call'd, and

the piper, as long as they are able to hold out; they that hold out longest at the exercise, win the cake and apples, and then the ale-wife's trade goes on. Pantomimic dances, to which allusions are also found, included the *Droghedy*, which was described as a very objectionable dance. *Maide na bPlanndaí*, performed in Connacht, was a solo dance in which the tilling, planting, and digging of the potato was imitated.

Only a few of these pantomimic or action dances have survived into the present century. Of these, *Rince an Chlaidhimh* is met with most frequently, but in a debased or simplified version. Sweeping-brushes, shovels or spades, sticks, chalked lines, or even a bow laid across a fiddle replace the swords of the seventeenth century. In Cork and Waterford this change is reflected in the change of title to *rince an chipín* and *step an chipín*. In Limerick the dance was called *Cover the Buckle* (this was the name of a step also) and in Clare, where it is still well known, *An Gabhairín Buí*. The latter name derives from the song *Tá dhá ghabhairín buí agam*, which is sung to a verion of *Hielan' Laddie*, the air to which the dance is usually performed in Clare.

The Clap Dance is rather a musical game than a dance. It was performed by two people who sat together or stood opposite each other. They started the performance by striking their own knees with the palms of their hands. Then they struck their partner's hands with their own in patterned combinations of movements. In the *Stick Dance*, as performed in Cavan, the dancer waved a stick in time to the music during the first strain of the tune, and then passed the stick under his legs and arms and around his body whilst keeping time to the music. This dance may well be a form of *rince an ghadaraigh* which has already been mentioned.

The Frog Dance, also called the *Cobbler's Dance*, is more an acrobatic feat than a dance. The performer crouches in a squatting posture, throws out his left foot with great vigour, withdraws it, repeats the action with his right, and proceeds in this somewhat grotesque manner around the floor. This dance or caper is known as *Damhsa na gCoinín* in Connemara.

III

Irish dancing reached the height of its perfection in the solo or step dances, the absence of references to which in the accounts of travellers who commented on the social scene in the eighteenth century would suggest that they are comparatively modern. The last quarter of the eighteenth century seems the most likely period for their invention, and there can be little doubt we owe their existence to the dancing masters. The principal step dances are the jig, reel, and hornpipe.

The common or double jig is the most popular of these. It was performed usually by one couple, but the number was not restricted. It commences with the 'rising step', the first step the learner is taught. One form of this step is performed by throwing the right foot forward about twelve inches above the floor, hopping on the left, while the right is withdrawn to tap the floor, and then tapping with the left, right and left foot. This action, occupying one bar of the tune, is repeated three times. To the fourth or last bar of the phrase the boy performed the *grinding step* on his left foot, the girl the *shuffle*. Grinding is performed by striking the floor with the toes of each foot alternately in time to the six notes in the bar, shuffling by giving each foot alternately a light shuffling motion in front of the other. In Limerick it was considered unladylike for a girl to do the grinding step or any of the other heavy or robust battering and drumming steps performed by the boy. Following the rising step and shuffling the girl changed

43

to graceful sliding steps modelled on the shuffle. Each step or movement was more elaborate than its predecessor and was completed with the shuffle. The men's steps followed practically the same sequence but were more intricate, with grinding, battering, and drumming being introduced in all kinds of combinations.

In this jig the battering step is doubled and is called 'doubled battering', or simply 'doubling', from which the dance gets its name. This movement begins by the dancer placing the weight of the body on one foot and giving a slight hop. Then the other foot is thrown forward, the floor being struck with the ball of the foot, whereupon this foot is immediately withdrawn, the floor being struck again during the backward movement. The floor is thus struck three times, with a hop in one foot and double tapping with the other, in time with the three quavers of the bar. This action may be continued right through, but more frequently it is blended with other movements. Drumming is performed by toe and heel in time to the triplet, and may be continued for a considerable time, or, like the battering, combined with other movements. An extraordinary number of intricate and complicated steps were based on the basic shuffling, grinding, skipping, drumming, and battering movements. It is recorded that in a contest between two dancing masters one performed thirty-six distinct steps, only to be beaten by his rival, who performed a further six!

The single jig is not unlike the double, but is modified to suit the crotchet-quaver arrangement of the music. Thus, in grinding, the floor is struck only four times instead of six (as in the double jig), and in battering only twice—by the hop on the first foot and a tap on the forward movement of the other foot. It is this single battering which gives the tune its name.

The hop or slip jig, the most graceful of the step dances, is performed to a tune of like name in 9/8 time. The steps consist of light hopping, tripping, and sliding actions, whence its description as a hop or slip jig. It was usually danced by two couples, but the numbers were not restricted since each couple danced independently of the others. As in the reel, only the alternate parts of the tune were danced or stepped. During the other parts of the tune the dancers promenaded around the room or stage in a light skipping movement, returning to their own places to begin the next step.

Some country dances, e.g. *Sir Roger de Coverly*, were formerly danced to this measure, and the tunes were so much more numerous in Ireland than in either England or Scotland that the steps used in them were known in England as Irish steps.

The reel, which after the double jig is the most popular of the step dances, is performed like the hop jig, the steps of the dance alternating with a promenade, each of these movements occupying one part or eight bars of the music. In some cases, instead of moving around the room on the completion of a step, a movement called a side step is substituted.

The hornpipe was usually danced by one man alone. It was rarely danced by a woman, as the steps were regarded as requiring the vigour and sound which only a man could bring to them. It appears the ladies of Cork were exceptional in that they not alone danced the hornpipe, but used the heavier steps in jigs and reels which elswhere were used exclusively by men.

IV

In the early years of the last century, the round or group dances comprised country dances and figure dances based on the solo reel and jig. The country dances mentioned as being in vogue towards the end of the seventeenth century seem to have disappeared, but the *rince fada* was still being performed, though not in the form in which it was supposed to have been danced to welcome James II. The reel of three, and the reel of four or the common reel, appear to have been the first of what would nowadays be described as 'céilí' dances. These were later followed by the eight-hand reel, *High Caul Cap*, sixteen-hand reel, *Humours of Bandon*, and the other round and figure dances, familiar to all who have attended *céilíthe* organised by Connradh na Gaeilge, which popularised those dances some seventy years ago.

Intervening between the age of the reel-of-three and the common reel and that of the later céilí dances were the sets and half sets which were the most popular dances throughout the country in the last and present century. In their many localised forms all these derive from the quadrille, a dance in which couples faced each other in the form of a square (whence the name). Quadrilles were tremendously popular in the Paris of Napoleon. The victorious armies of Wellington became familiar with them and later introduced them to England and Ireland. The then Knight of Glin, it is said, ordered the dancing masters of the district to teach the new dances as they were performed in France and Spain. The dancing masters, however, adapted these dances by substituting native steps for the ball-room steps and by speeding up the time to that of the jig and common reel.

Thus naturalised, the sets of quadrilles (shortened to 'sets' and so called when four couples took part, and to 'half sets' when two couples danced) spread throughout the country and maintained their popularity for over a hundred years. Differences developed in the number of

46

figures (which ranged from three to six, the usual number being five) and in their execution, and local names were used for the variants which emerged. These included the plain or common set, *Calendonian*, *Paris*, *Orange and Green*, the reel set, the jig set, the *Cashel*, *Ballycommon*, and *Ballysteen*.

The five figures of the original quadrilles required music in 6/8 and 2/4 time, in which a great deal of native music was already being played, so that, with the step adaptations already mentioned, there were no real obstacles to the assimilation of the newly imported sets. Their sustained and widespread popularity was, without doubt, responsible for keeping alive a great deal of native dance music. In view of this it is somewhat ironic that these dances in all their variant forms were later to be declared 'foreign' and banished from the social activities of revivalists in favour of *céilí* dances which almost certainly had been devised by the Munster dancing masters on the pattern of the quadrilles.

V

The word *céilí*, in a usage common in northern districts, means a gathering of neighbours in the evening in some house where talk and gossip on matters of local interest help to put in the night. This custom, in Anglo-Irish speech called *kayleeing*, is in Clare and elsewhere spoken of as 'making a cuaird', and no musical entertainment or dancing is implied. To describe an organised dance as a *céilí* then was a misnomer, but one which in fact served to emphasise the social nature of the gathering. Strangely enough, the first *céilí* organised by the newly founded Connradh na Gaeilge, or Gaelic League, was held not in Ireland but in London—in the Bloomsbury Hall near the

British Museum on 30 October, 1897. Organised by the London branch, of which Fionán Mac Coluim, afterwards editor of *Cosa Buí Arda* and other collections of songs in Irish, was an active member, the programme included, besides stepdancing, music, and song, sets and waltzes performed to Irish airs! A form of group dancing was devised by having boys and girls face each other in two lines to perform the double jig. Between each step the facing couples changed places by a linking movement, so that only every second step was danced in the dancers' original position. In this way a movement was achieved which superficially at any rate looked like the group dances performed by the Scots at their functions in London. *Rincí Gaelacha* in the strict sense had not yet arrived.

5. The Dancing Master

> . . . *the old dancing master had some very marked outlines of character peculiar to himself.*
>
> —WILLIAM CARLETON in *The Country Dancing Master.*

THE dancing master as a figure in the social life of the countryside appears on the scene in the second half of the eighteenth century. Arthur Young in his account of his travels in Ireland in the years 1776 to 1779 remarked that dancing was so universal among the poor people that dancing masters travelled through the country from cabin to cabin, with a piper or blind fiddler, and were paid by the cottiers for teaching their children dancing. This national recreation, Young declared to be an absolute system of education.

Descriptions of the dancing master in the early years of the last century portray a somewhat whimsical figure, pretentious in dress and affecting a grandiloquence not sustained by his schooling. Caroline hat, swallow-tail coat and tight knee-breeches, white stockings and turn-pumps, cane with a silver head and silk tassell—thus accoutered the dancing master was obviously a cut above the wandering piper or fiddler. He was a person to be treated with due deference by his pupils. Good carriage and deportment were his by profession. He considered himself a gentleman, conducted himself as one, and endeavoured to instil this spirit into his best pupils.

The arrival of the dancing master at village or hamlet was hailed with delight, for his advent ensured music and dancing for six weeks at least. His first move on arrival was to arrange with a farmer to let him have the use of a kitchen or barn. Occasionally an unused house or other building might be available for the lessons. In one or two places a rudely built edifice, roofed with scraws, was erected by the local people for the purpose. In Kerry, it was not uncommon to hold the dancing school in conjunction with a hedge school, the different classes being conducted simultaneously at either end of the premises. It was even said of some places in that county that it was pointless to attempt holding a hedge school unless a class for dancing was held with it. More often than not the dancing master stayed with the farmer from whom he had received a place for his class, and in return taught the children of the house both music and dancing gratis. Otherwise, the pupils in turn brought him home for the night, vieing with each other for this honour.

Although an itinerant, the dancing master moved within a well defined territory, a district perhaps of ten square miles. A friendly rivalry existed between all dancing masters and each respected the other's territory. Casual meetings at fairs and sporting events would lead to challenges when both would dance it out in public to the joy and edification of the spectators and, frequently, without any eventual decision. Occasionally, the event demanded a victor, as when a Kerry dancing master vanquished a Cork dancing master in a contest as to who should 'own' Clonmel. A stranger at Callan seeing a large and attentive crowd looking at two dancers performing alternately on the soaped head of an upturned barrel was informed, on enquiring what was going on, that the two were dancing masters 'wieing' for the parish.

The dancing master did not confine his activities to teaching dancing. He was always qualified to teach deportment and was sometimes engaged to teach that subject to the children of the well-to-do, without dancing lessons or perhaps with lessons in waltzing or dancing quadrilles. The dancing master, like the piper or fiddler, did not restrict himself solely to the native dances.

In the early decades of the nineteenth century many dancing masters professed a further accomplishment. Fencing schools, more precisely to be styled cudgel-playing, were as common then as the dancing school, and it was not unusual to find the same person in charge of both.

The earliest references to the remuneration of the dancing master indicate that he received a quarterly fee from his scholars. In Young's day the fee was six-pence. In Wexford around 1816 pupils had to pay the master a 'thirteen' (there were thirteen Irish pence in a British shilling) and a tester (sixpence-halfpenny) to the fiddler for a quarter of nine nights. It seems, how-ever, that the dancing master's quarter was more commonly one of six weeks, and over the years the fee naturally varied. Towards the middle of the last century the charge in Kerry was 10/– per quarter, 5/– for the dancing master and 5/– for the musician. The pupils, however, received two 'benefit' nights, the first a fortnight and the second a month after the com-mencement of the class. On these occasions the teacher and the musician in turn bought drink (a half tierse of porter) for the entertainment of their pupils. Outsiders attending the benefit were expected to make a con-tribution towards the expenses. Exceptionally, the dancing master enjoyed the benefit. He announced the holding of a benefit night during which he took up a collection for himself. Payments were sometimes made at a weekly rate, occasionally at so much a step.

The rising step was the first step of the jig which was taught, the side step in the case of the reel. With the mastery of these two steps, progress was rapid, but the difficulty was in mastering them. A universal problem confronting the dancing master, it seems, was the inability of his pupils to distinguish their right from their left, and hay and straw or withies were attached to the pupils' feet so that they could more easily follow the oral directions of the master. Terms like 'hayrope' and 'straw rope', or 'hay foot' and 'straw foot', were used by all the dancing masters, and jingles incorporating them were devised for teaching the elementary steps:

> Sín amach cos an ghaid agus crap cos an tsúgáin,
> Bain cnag as t'altaibh agus searradh as do
> ghlúnaibh;
> Síos go dtí an doras agus suas go dtí an cúinne
> Is go mbris' an riabhach do chosa mara deacair
> tú do mhúineadh.

(Stretch out the withie foot and withdraw the strawrope foot/ Take a crack out of your joints and a stretch out of your knees/Down to the door and up to the corner/ and may the devil break your feet if you are not hard to teach.)

This jingle was obviously delivered to the strains of *Miss McLeod's Reel*. 'Rise on sugan an' sink upon gad', used for teaching the jig step, suited *The Campbells are coming*, the same air as *Miss McLeod* but played in jig time.

The reputation of the dancing master rested no less on his power of execution, or indeed of inventing the intricate steps of the solo dances, than on his ability to teach them. The solo dances—the basic reel and jig—

and the special set or figure dances (e.g., *The Blackbird*, *Bonaparte's Retreat*, and *St. Patrick's Day*) were the creation of the dancing masters, but in only one case is the name of a dancing master associated with a set dance, *The Blackbird* being said to have been composed by Keily, a Limerick dancing master, over 150 years ago. Because of the skill and practice required for their correct performance, the solo dances were held in most esteem, and often the trap or half door was taken down off its hinges, or the table cleared, in order to provide a suitable platform for a good solo dancer.

The less gifted and more numerous members of the company found an outlet for their high spirits in the round or group dances, which, it is said, were devised by the dancing masters to maintain the interest of their less ardent pupils and afford couples an opportunity for colloguing. The standard of performance in these more sociable dances was no mean one either, since all the dancers had been taught the basic steps of the jig and the reel.

A remarkable feature of step dancing was the control or restraint which underlay the vigour and speed of the performance. The good dancer kept the body rigid, moving only from the hips down and with arms extended straight at the side. This restrained type of dancing was apparently the ideal of the dancing masters who discouraged flinging the hands about, or flourishing them at the level of the head, as well as the cutting of such acrobatic steps as *léim an bhradáin* (the salmon leap). The good dancer, it was said, could dance on eggs without breaking them and hold a pan of water on his head without spilling a drop, and these fanciful descriptions underline the disciplined movements favoured by the dancing masters. The good dancer danced, as it were, underneath himself, trapping each note of the music on the floor, and the use of the half door and table for solo performances indicates the limited area in which he was expected to perform the elaborate and intricate steps.

The dancing master survived into the present century. To two of them in particular we owe the recovery of many of our figure dances. O'Keeffe and O'Brien, the authors of *A Hand Book of Irish Dances* (1902)—the standard work on the subject—obtained from Patrick Reidy, an old Kerry dancing master then living in London, the *rinnce fada*, the four- and eight-hand reels, and *The High Caul Cap*. Tomás Sheáin Ó Súilleabháin, of Glenbeigh, Co. Kerry, contributed the twelve- and sixteen-hand reels and *The Humours of Bandon*. Fionán Mac Coluim, from whom the information here and elsewhere about céilí dancing derives, translated the title of *The Humours of Bandon* as *Pléaráca na Bandan!* Go ndéana Dia Grásta orthu ar fad.

Reidy, or Professor Reidy as he styled himself, had learnt his dancing from his own father, who in turn had been a pupil of the great O'Kearin, a Kerry dancing master who flourished at the end of the eighteenth century. O'Kearin is reputed to have imparted to the basic step dances the order and style which obtained throughout the whole country.

6. The Dance Music

Even the very lame and blind
If trump or bagpipe they do hear
In dancing posture do appear.
　　　　—The Irish Hudibras, 1728

I

THE popularity of dancing is often mentioned in the accounts of seventeenth- and eighteenth-century Ireland written by the visiting scribes. An Englishman, Richard Head, in a work entitled *The Western Wonder* (1674), says of the Sunday amusements: 'in every field a fiddle and the lasses footing it till they are all of a foam'. An almost identical observation is made by another English traveller, John Carr, in his *Stranger in Ireland* (1805): 'A Sunday with the peasantry in Ireland is not unlike the same day in France. After the hours of devotion, a spirit of gaiety shines upon every hour, the bagpipe is heard, and every foot is in motion.' In the latter half of the eighteenth century every group of cabins, we are told, had its own piper and its own schoolmaster, and every countryman had his halfpenny for the piper on Sunday afternoon.

Expert tuition was available everywhere and within reach of all with the arrival of the travelling dancing master. In an era when commercial dance halls or indeed, halls of any kind were unknown, and most travelling was done on foot, dancing was the social pastime, and it was indulged in at crossroads or on a *móinín* (a green grassy patch) when the weather was kind, or in kitchens and barns during the winter.

Innumerable musicians—trump players, harpers and bagpipers in the seventeenth century, pipers and fiddlers in the eighteenth century—provided the music. Many of the musicians were blind, or otherwise physically incapacitated, and music offered them a respectable and respected living.

From all this activity we have inherited an immensely rich legacy of dance music. Although now being eroded unceasingly since the beginning of the century, this body of music still contains, at a conservative estimate, over 6,000 individual pieces—jigs, reels, and hornpipes in profusion, and hundreds of tunes for sets and half sets, polkas and other dances.

With the exception of a score or so of tunes to which special dances are performed, all these tunes share a similar structure. Each consists of at least two strains or parts of eight bars—there are no dance tunes and only very few airs which have only one strain. In the vast majority of tunes each part is made up of two phrases. The common pattern is a single phrase repeated with some slight modification, with the phrases falling naturally into half-phrases of two bars each. A basic element present alike in song and dance music is exhibited in these half-phrases; the first making, as it were, an assertion to which the second is the response. This principle of contrast is present to some extent even between the two phrases of a strain, although as suggested, the melodic differences, if any, may be only slight.

It is now usual to repeat each part of single and double jigs, hornpipes, and the music for sets. The parts of the slip jig are played only once, while the method of playing the reel varies. Formerly the reel was played single to match the dance, but now, when the music is played more often for listening to than for dancing, it is customary to double the reel, that is, to play each part twice over, unless the two phrases which comprise a part are identical or almost so, in which case, to avoid monotony, that part is singled or played only once. In some reels, following this practice, it may happen that one part is played twice, another part only once. One reel, bearing the curious title *The Nine Points of Roguery* and almost certainly a migrant, has its three parts repeated, but performed in the unusual order of 1 2 3 2 1 2. Among practitioners the first part of a piece is known as the 'tune' and the second as the 'turn'. Whence the story of the local priest who, having dispersed the dancers at a crossroad gathering, asked the blind-musician, with heavy sarcasm, whether he could play the Our Father. The musician replied that if his reverence would whistle the tune, he was sure he would be able to turn it for him.

II

The jig, which is the oldest form of dance music surviving, is found in three forms: the single jig (in 6/8 and occasionally in 12/8 time); the double (in 6/8 time); and the hop or slip jig (in 9/8 time). The word 'jig' undoubtedly derives from the Italian, and it has been suggested that the music itself may also have an Italian origin, coming here from Italy through the harpers. This idea derives from the fact that Carolan, who was fascinated by the Italian music in vogue in his time in Dublin, concluded some of his compositions with a piece of sixteen bars to which the title *jiga* was prefixed. But the only similarity between these pieces and the native dance music is in the number of bars, and they differ so radically in structure and idiom that one may dismiss the idea that one derives from the other. Apart from that, however, we have a reference to the dancing of jigs in Ireland when Carolan was a child of four. Dr. Peter Talbot, Archbishop of Dublin, attacking Friar Peter Walsh, the leader of the Catholics who were willing to adopt a remonstrance of loyalty to Charles II, refers to the friar and his followers in a passage which is worth quoting at length:

> Call you *suffering*, to see these your spiritual Children return home to you with money in their purses, and treat you and your Commissary, very splendidly at the sign of the Harp and Croun in Dublin, almost euery night, with good Cheer, dancing, and *Danes*, or Irish *Cronans*; especially that famous *Macquillemone*; which was stiled in a letter to Rome, *Cantio barbara & aggrestis*; and call'd by the Soldiors of the Guards in Dublin (hearing it euery night at midnight) Friar Walsh, and Friar N. singing of Psalmes? Call you *suffering* to see your graue Remonstrants dance Giggs and Countrey dances, to recreat your-self and the Commissary, who was as ready and nimble at it, as any of his Collectors? but indeed its said, you danc't with a better grace than any of the Company.

— *The Friar Disciplin'd*, 1674

Moreover, tunes similar to our jigs were in circulation in England long before Italian music became popular in these islands. Melodically, of course, the great bulk of our Irish jigs are native in origin. Some few are undoubtedly borrowed from the English, scarcely any from the Scots. The older ones may have been derived from ancient clan marches and songs, and some, perhaps, were adapted from older dance tunes. The vast majority, however, appear to have been composed by the pipers and fiddlers of the eighteenth and nineteenth centuries.

Seven bars, each containing two triplets of quavers, and an eighth or concluding bar containing a triplet of quavers followed by a crotchet, is the usual form of the double jig. The time of the last bar is completed by the introductory note of the succeeding part. It is quite common for the second and third quavers in the eighth bar to be the same pitch as the following crotchet. The pattern, however, is not rigid. Rhythmical variations occur in all bars, in some cases with subtle changes in accenting. The form of the single jig differs from that of the double jig in that the first seven bars usually consist of two groups each comprising a crotchet and quaver. Frequently a group is displaced by a triplet of quavers. The eighth or last bar of the part almost invariably follows a dotted crotchet and crotchet formula, with the time of the bar completed, as in the double jig, by the introductory note of the succeeding part.

The hop or slip jig is in 9/8 time, the bars being filled by various groupings of triplets of quavers, crotchet and quavers, and dotted crotchets. It is very common for the last bar of the part to be so constructed as to run into the succeeding part. Rhythmical differences between types of this jig suggest basic differences in the steps of the dances formerly performed to this measure. Petrie expressed the opinion that the hop jig evolved from a class of ancient Irish vocal melodies and was peculiar to this country. Whatever about the origin of the native tunes, it is not correct to say that this type of dance tune is peculiar to Ireland. Undoubtedly this measure had an extraordinary vogue here—some hundreds of pieces have been collected—but the early English printed collections abound in 9/8 tunes which, to borrow a phrase from Petrie himself, are 'of sturdy English sentiment' and cannot be claimed on any ground as being Irish or of Irish origin.

The reel, now the favourite dance tune among traditional players, is, in its present form at least, not very much older than the hornpipe, and appears to have evolved around the middle of the eighteenth century. Its parts consist of eight bars, each containing two groups of four quavers. Frequently the ending bar concludes in a crotchet or dotted crotchet, but a circular ending devised to go straight into the following part is not uncommon.

A very strong case can be made for ascribing a Scots ancestry to our reels. The collections of dance music published in London in the second half of the seventeenth century and the first half of the eighteenth century contain tunes of Irish origin, jigs in 6/8 and 9/8 time, some of which may still be heard among traditional players. There is an abundance of these tunes in the Irish collections which appeared in the closing decades of the eighteenth century, whereas tunes which would be regarded nowadays as reels are scarcely represented in either the early London or later Dublin collections. On the other hand, the music sheets printed in Dublin towards the end of the century carry what are obviously Scottish reels, and perhaps *Lord McDonald* and *Miss McLeod* owe their popularity in Ireland to their inclusion on some of these sheets.

What seems to clinch the matter, however, is the fact that many of our great reels are undoubtedly Scottish, and they can, in fact, be attributed to known composers, *Bonnie Kate*, a particular favourite among fiddle players because of the highly decorative setting in which the Sligo fiddle player, Michael Coleman, played it, was composed by Daniel Dow, a fiddler from Perthshire. It was first published around 1760 under the name of *The Bonnie Lass of Fisherrow*. Dow also composed *Bonnie Anne*, better known here in the variant to which *Follow me down to Carlow* is sung; whilst *Moneymusk*, another of Dow's compositions, was a popular tune in Ireland for the Highland Fling.

Among the numerous compositions of William Marshall, another Scots violinist, was *The Duke of Gordon's Rant*, which in a highly developed form is known among pipers and fiddlers in Ireland as *Lord Gordon's Reel*. *The Perthshire Hunt*, composed by Miss Stirling of Ardoch, and published for the first time in 1780, is usually called *The Boyne Hunt* in Ireland. Its popularity here is attested by the other sixty or more titles by which it is also known. *The Fairy Reel* does not belong to the *Ceol Sí* or fairy music. It was composed by Neil Gow for the Fife Hunt Ball held in 1802, and became so Irish that a special dance *Cor na Sióga* is performed to it.

Other favourite reels which have been borrowed from Scotland are *Rakish Paddy* (there known as *Cabar Féigh* or *The Deer's Horn*), *John Frank* (*Colonel McBain*), *Greig's Pipes*, *Lucy Campbell*, *The Ranting Widow* (*Hopetoun House*), and *The Flogging Reel*. During their sojourn here, now bordering on 200 years, these and many other reels of Scottish origin have become naturalised. They have, indeed, flourished, as will be evident on a comparison of the versions current among Irish musicians with the original settings found in the eighteenth-century Scots collections.

The hornpipe has a structure similar to that of the reel, but it is played in a more deliberate manner, with a well defined accent on the first and third beats of each bar. Three accented crotchets is a feature of the closing bar of each part. The hornpipe is of English origin, and it assumed its present form around 1760, when it changed over from triple time (3/2) to common time. It was introduced on the stage at the time, and was danced between the acts and scenes of plays. The native melodies adapted to this dance tend to be more closely knit than the imported tunes, proceeding stepwise rather than by skips or jumps.

Set or long dances are solo dances, usually with a jig or hornpipe rhythm. They deviate generally from the usual form of the dance tune in having one part, usually the second, longer than the others, and sometimes the parts may be in different times. Each tune has its own particular dance which, following the usual Irish custom, has the same title. Transcriptions of two, *The Hunt* and *An Súisín Bán* are on pages 141–2. *St. Patrick's Day*, *The Blackthorn Stick*, *The Blackbird*, and *The Garden of Daisies* are other well known set dances. These were known as table dances in West Limerick; they required an expert to perform them properly, and his skill was exhibited much better on the kitchen table than it would have been on the clay floor of the house.

It was fortunate that when quadrilles were introduced into Ireland the musicians preferred the native tunes to those included in the numerous selections issued on the printed music sheets. Many of these composed pieces may be found in manuscript collections, but very few of them were adopted and retained in the tradition. Instead, the jigs and reels already current were used, and as time went on a great deal of other native music, such as marches and song airs, was treated somewhat rudely to shape it for the sets and half sets based on the quadrilles. Tunes in 6/8 time as used for the sets usually lack the close texture of the double jig and its contrasting half phrases. A tremendous body of music in 4/4 and 2/4 time developed for these dances. These tunes, of which those in 4/4 time are known in Clare as single reels, have a boldly accented rhythm with a pleasant melodic jingle and on that account would serve admirably as an introduction to the music for the learner.

The occurrence in manuscript collections of dance tunes having six, seven, or some other unusual number of bars in each strain points to the existence of dances different from these described above and now lost.

Transcriptions of the various types of dance music described in this chapter appear on pages 133 to 142.

III

The titles of dance tunes call for a comment or two. Titles have no musical connection whatever with tunes; they are merely labels used for ready identification. It is nonsense to suppose that *The Irish Washerwoman* in some mystical manner represents the strange personality of that now ancient lady, or that one may determine on hearing *The Mason's Apron* whether a stonemason's apron or a freemason's apron is implied by the title.

Occasionally, a title matches the rhythm of the last bar of a piece. There are four or five reels called *What the Devil ails You*, and one slip jig is known as *Cé thitfeadh sa tine nach n-éireodh?* These refrain-like phrases, suggested by the rhythm of the last bar, in all probability ousted older names. It is unlikely that they represent the endings of songs or refrains otherwise forgotten. The words associated with the rest of the strain could scarcely have been lost entirely. In *portaireacht* or *poirt bhéil*, in English jigging or lilting, which had to be resorted to when no instrumental music was available for dancing meaningless syllables were uttered to dance tunes, and the story is told of a lilter who missed being placed in a competition because he put in a 'doodle-dee' instead of a 'doodle-dum'. With the rapidity with which dancing was performed in Ireland however, it would scarcely have been possible to articulate the words of a song quickly enough for the dancers.

Titles like *The Rights of Man*, *Madame Bonaparte*, and *Bonaparte's Retreat*, as well as providing a pointer to the

63

period of their composition show on which side the sympathy of the people of Ireland lay in the revolutionary period, but these, together with *The Repeal of the Union*, *The Union is Welcome to Ireland*, and some titles incorporating the name of O'Connell, are among the few with historical associations. In general, the titles of our dance tunes afford no hint of the economic and social conditions of the times in which they were composed (though they do indicate that Jenny, Kitty, and Paddy appear to be the favourite Christian names). Again, the 'humours', as in *The Humours of Bandon*, though always associated with a place name and more commonly used with jigs than with reels, are obviously not intended to suggest diversions which are special to one particular place.

The Galway Reel may really be from Galway, or have been popular in that county, but, on the other hand, *The Fairy Reel* has nothing to do with the fairies. A personal name in the title almost invariably indicates a tune, the original name of which was lost, and which was later identified by the name of the player who popularised it. Exceptionally, the name indicates the composer. The names of hundreds of dance tunes have been lost, totally or in one or several districts. There are, however, three times as many titles as tunes, for some have half-a-dozen different titles, and *The Perthshire Hunt*, as already mentioned, has at least sixty other names. One cannot rely solely on the title to identify a tune, since identical names do not imply identical tunes. Thus there are at least half-a-dozen different tunes called *The Lark(s) on the Strand* and a like number of different *Geese in the Bog*.

7. Musical Instruments

The Irish Harp, whose rusty Mettle,
Sounds like the patching of a Kettle.
— *The Irish Hudibras*, 1689.

I

THE Harp. References to the *cruit* and to the magical effect of its music are numerous in the old stories, but no description of the instrument occurs which would permit a guess as to its form. The name *cruit* was applied to stringed instruments long before any kind of harp was known in north-western Europe, and it was applied to the instrument which emerged around the twelfth century as the distinctively Irish harp, although that differed in form from the harps depicted centuries previously on the old high crosses. *Cláirseach*, the modern term for the instrument, is found in fourteenth century verse. It has been suggested, somewhat fancifully, that in Scotland, where the two forms were also in use, *cláirseach* signified a harp strung with wire, and *cruit* signified a harp strung with gut or hair. Both words were seemingly interchangeable here, so that one may conclude that the later word did not come into use in Ireland to signify a development or change in the instrument.

The distinguishing feature of the Irish harp was its robust construction. The sound box was hollowed from a solid block of sally or willow; the fore-pillar was sturdy, curving outwards, and T-shaped in section, the top of the letter, as it were, facing outwards. The neck was deep and heavy and bound on either side with a metal band. The strings, which were of thick brass, were carried by metal pins on the left-hand side of the neck, the other ends being twisted around wooden pegs inside the sound box.

The so-called 'Brian Boru Harp', preserved in Trinity College Dublin, has been used as a model for the national emblem depicted on the coinage. This harp, which belongs to the fourteenth century, is the oldest surviving specimen of the native instrument, and is, besides, one of the few musical instruments which have survived more or less intact from medieval Europe. It was restrung some years ago with metal strings, and sounded in the old Irish manner with long crooked nails. The sound, we are told, was extraordinarily sweet 'and clear, with a quality which was somewhat bell-like but with an added richness akin to that of the guitar'. We have, then, some idea of the sound of the Irish harp, even if we do not possess any examples of the music played upon it.

The honoured place occupied by the harper in the political and cultural life of Gaelic Ireland is evidenced by the entries marking the death of harpers in the native annals. The Annals of Loch Cé record the death in 1225 of Aedh Ó Sochlachainn, Vicar of Cong, *saí canntairechta ocus crotglesa, maroen re gles do denum do féin nach dernadh remhe* (professor of singing and harp tuning who invented a tuning for himself not previously made); and the Annals of Ulster mention the death in the year 1496 of Florence Corcoran, *sai cruitire & fhir thed & fer budh roibhind do bel & do laimh* (a master harper and instrumentalist, a man melodious in singing and in playing). Many harpers, too, are mentioned in the English State Papers, where their names are recorded as those of criminals who had received the royal pardon.

We are dependent entirely on outside sources for the

meagre knowledge we possess about the kind of music played by the harpers, as the early musicians made no use of any form of musical notation to preserve their music, nor did they think it worth their while to describe it. Giraldus Cambrensis has left us in his *Topographia Hiberniae* an account of his visits to Ireland in 1183 and 1185. He found nothing about the inhabitants to praise except their skill on musical instruments, which, he declared, was incomparably superior to that of any other nation. In a much quoted and somewhat obscure passage he described the music as quick and articulate, but nevertheless sweet and pleasing in sound. He was amazed at the perfection with which the rhythm was maintained during passages of the most rapid fingerwork, and at the way in which the melody was preserved throughout the most complicated rhythm and involved polyphony.

In contrasting Irish and British music, Giraldus refers only to the style of playing, and in describing the artistry of the Irish musicians he draws attention to the refinement of his own musical appreciation. This, and the absence of any reference to its being in any way exotic, indicates that the music he heard in Ireland was of the kind played at the centres of learning and culture on the Continent and with which he would have been acquainted. As we have seen the harper also engaged in another form of music-making, when with the *reacaire* or bard he joined in the presentation of the official verse which the *file* or official poet composed to record the chief events in the life of his prince or chief.

It is only towards the end of the eighteenth century, when the harp was on the verge of extinction, that we have any account of the lives of harpers. By then they had degenerated into itinerant musicians with a repertoire for the most part composed of folk airs and the planxties and other compositions of Carolan. The blind nonogenarian, Denis Hempson, was the only one of the ten harpers present at the Belfast Festival in 1792 who played in the traditional manner, with long crooked finger nails on strings of brass. Arthur O'Neill, another blind harper who attended the Festival dictated his memoirs at the instance of Edward Bunting and this account and Bunting's own observations constitute the slender store of knowledge we possess about the last of the Irish harpers.

Efforts were made after the Belfast festival to have some blind boys taught the instrument, but these

H. O'Neill, A.H.R.A.

FIGURE 11. James Gandsey, King of the Kerry pipers.

proved unavailing. The frayed and wasted link, joining these poor, blind, itinerant harpers with the professional artists who had so excited Giraldus in the twelfth century, parted in the opening decades of the nineteenth and the old traditional manner of harping passed into oblivion.

II

THE PIPES. *Pípaí, fidlí, fir cen gail, cnámfhir agus cuisleannaig* (bagpipes, fiddles, men of no valour, bone players, and pipe blowers) were part of the entertainment provided at the Fair of Carman, according to a poet writing around the middle of the eleventh century, that is, in pre-Norman Ireland. As already mentioned this reference, and others elsewhere, indicate a distinction between the *píopaí* and the *cuisleanna ceoil*. Some centuries later the word *píopaí* undoubtedly signified bagpipes, as it does in the modern language. The borrowing of the new word would indicate the introduction of a new instrument or at least the modification of one already in use. It seems safe, therefore, to take it the bagpipe was known in eleventh century Ireland and this would be in line with the history of the instrument in medieval times. The earliest mention of it occurs in the ninth century; by the eleventh century pipes had spread like wildfire throughout western Europe. It is not until the late fifteenth or early sixteenth century that we find a representation of the bagpipes relating to this country. A rude wood carving of a piper formerly in Woodstock Castle, Co. Kilkenny, belongs to this period. A drawing of a youth playing the pipes on the margin of a missal which had belonged to the abbey of Rosgall, Co. Kildare, cannot be much later in date. The pipes depicted in these representations comprise chanter, bag and two drones, similar to those depicted about

69

this time in continental Europe, for example, the piper of Dürer dated 1514. They are, of course, the prototype of the *píob mór* or war pipes of the present-day pipers' bands. The third drone was added in Scotland early in the last century to complete what is now regarded as the full set.

FIGURE 12. A pig performing on the pipes from a sixteenth-century MS. in the Royal Irish Academy.

While references to wars and forays are numerous in the old stories and chronicles, there is no indication that the pipes or, indeed, any other musical instrument were used in battle in pre-Norman Ireland. In Tudor Ireland, however, the piper was part of the military establishment. Pipers accompanied the kernes who were employed by Henry VIII in his wars against the Scots and the French; they were present at the siege of Boulogne in 1544, and a contemporary painting showed a party of Irish kernes, led by a piper, returning to camp after a *creach* or cattle raid. In 1572, the Lord Deputy writing from Dublin, complains to Elizabeth

that Fiach Mac Aodha Ó Broin, Rúairí Óg Ó Mórdha
and other rebels were so disdainful of the weakened
defences of the Pale that they came on their raids
headed by pipers in the daytime and by torch-bearers
at night, and an illustration in a contemporary work,
Derricke's *Image of Irelande* (1581), affords a vivid
picture of such a scene (Fig. 13). A French traveller
in the middle of the following century observed that
the Irish marched to battle with the bagpipes, but that
they had few drums.

The pipes were also in use at funerals. A traveller in

FIGURE 13. Piper leading kerne from Derricke's *Image of Irelande*,
1581.

sixteenth-century Ireland wrote: 'With it also they
accompany·their dead to the grave, making such
mournful sounds as to invite, nay almost force the
bystanders to weep'. On more enjoyable occasions,
however, the pipes were also in demand. 'At hurling',

writes another English traveller, Dunton, towards the end of the century, 'two or three bagpipers attend the conquerors at the barrell's head (the prize for the winning team) and they play them off the field'.

It is almost certain that the many references we find to the bagpipes down to the end of the seventeenth century relate to what are now called the war pipes, and the emergence of a distinctively Irish instrument is usually placed in the early decades of the following century. Its distinguishing features, initially, were a chanter having a range of two octaves as compared with one of nine notes on the older pipes, and the use of a bellows instead of blowpipe to inflate the bag. The full set of modern times comprises a bag, bellows and chanter, drones and regulators. These Irish pipes, known variously as Union and *Uilleann*, or more simply among practitioners as *na píopaí*, the pipes, are regarded as outstanding among the pipes of the world for their highly developed state and singular sweetness of tone. The bag is made from basan popularly called bazil, a soft dry-cured sheepskin. Rubber and other materials are sometimes used, but are not entirely satisfactory. Box and ebony were most in favour for making the body of the pipes, with fittings of silver or brass and ivory. Box is now seldom used and, instead, African hardwood and other close-grained woods are used as well as ebony.

The chanter—the pipe on which the melody is played —has a range of two octaves extending upwards from the D above the middle C of the piano, in the case of pipes in concert pitch. The pitch of the chanter is largely determined by its length. A chanter 36 cm in length will sound in concert pitch, one 40 cm in length a note below that. In the older sets the pitch is usually a tone, sometimes more, below concert pitch, but sets in the latter pitch are now the general rule.

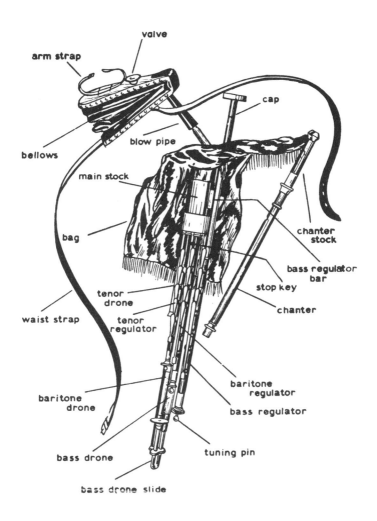

FIGURE 14. A modern set of Irish pipes.

73

Conventionally, the bottom or fundamental note of the chanter is called D irrespective of its pitch. Similarly, the bottom note of a flute or a whistle is also called D irrespective of its actual pitch. The system of fingering is shown hereunder. A full range of chromatic intervals can be secured on the chanter by the provision of keys, and many chanters are, at least partly, fitted in this manner. Since the music avoids the use of chromatic semitones these keys serve no particular purpose except in the case of one note, viz. C natural; it is difficult without a key to sound C natural in the second octave. This is the only instance in which the music demands such assistance.

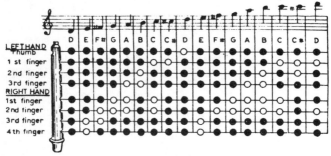

FIGURE 15. Range and fingering of chanter. ● ○ denote, respectively, holes to be covered or left open. Except when sounding the bottom note, the chanter is normally rested on a small pad of leather worn by the piper above the right knee. This pad, known as the popping strap, makes the chanter air-tight when all the vents are covered by the fingers. Its use is essential for crisp non-legato playing and for securing a bright, clear tone, particularly in the second octave. A valve fitted to the bottom of the chanter is sometimes used instead of the strap. Variations in fingering occur in rapid playing and when the chanter is raised off the knee. C natural is usually obtained in the second octave with the aid of a key which is fitted to the back of the chanter and operated by the lower thumb.

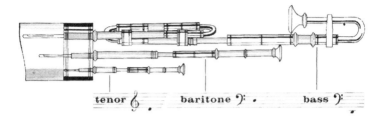

FIGURE 16. Drones of the Irish pipes.

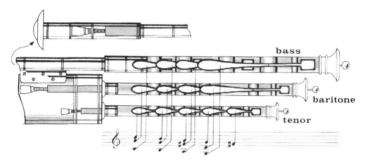

FIGURE 17. Regulators of the Irish pipes.

The upper octave is obtained on the chanter by overblowing, that is by exerting additional pressure on the bag, and it is one of the arts of the piper to do this without affecting the tone of the drones which are sounding below the melody.

The drones, numbering three in a full set, sound a continuous unchanging accompaniment to the chanter. The tenor, or small drone is tuned to the bottom note of the chanter, the baritone or midde drone being tuned an octave, and the bass or long drone a further octave, below that note (Fig. 16). The regulators, also three in number in the full set, are stopped pipes fitted with keys. The tenor or small

75

regulator sounds the notes F♯, G, A, B, and C in unison with the chanter. The baritone or middle regulator sounds D, F ♯, G, and A in unison with the chanter, and the bass or large regulator sounds the notes G to C an octave below these notes on the tenor regulator (Fig. 17). The three regulators are so arranged beneath the bottom hand of the performer that simple chords to accompany the chanter can be achieved by depressing the keys with the lower edge of the hand and the wrist, thus permitting the regulators to sound. A change from this straight-across accompaniment can be achieved only when the bottom hand of the performer is free, that is when the chanter is sounding from G to D¹ (i.e. the notes played by the top hand) in either octave. It was the custom among pipers to play slow airs without any accompaniment, even that of the drones. If anything, the regulators tend to be over-used nowadays, being used particularly in dance music rather more as a rhythmical than a harmonic accompaniment.

The instrument is constantly referred to as the 'uilleann' pipes, but the correct name is 'union', and the pipes are so styled by O'Farrell, who provided the earliest known tutor for the instrument in his *Collection of National Irish Music for the Union Pipes* (*c.* 1800). The surmise that the instrument derived its name from the Act of Union (1800) because it was assuming its fully developed form about that time can be dismissed, as the name occurs in a poem of 1796 describing the rivalry between two music sellers 'in fair Cork town', where one Fitzpatrick at the Harp is extolled:

For he can play the Union Pipes
And nobly squeeze his bags.

—*The Rover*, 5 March, 1796

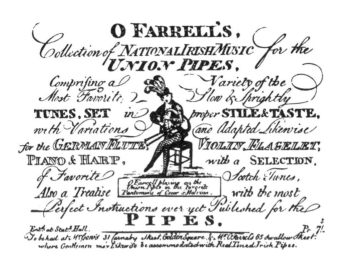

O FARRELL'S,
Collection of NATIONAL IRISH MUSIC for the
UNION PIPES,
Comprising a *Variety of the*
Most Favorite, *Slow & Sprightly*
TUNES, SET *in* *proper* **STILE & TASTE,**
with Variations *and Adapted Likewise*
for the **GERMAN FLUTE,** **VIOLIN, FLAGELET,**
PIANO & HARP, *with a* **SELECTION,**
of Favorite *Scotch Tunes,*
Also a Treatise *with the most*
Perfect Instructions ever yet Published for the
PIPES.

Enter'd at Stat.? Hall. Pr. 7/.
To behad at M.? Gow's 31 Carnaby Street, Golden Square &, M.? O'Farrels 65 Swallow Street,
where Gentlemen may Likewise be accommodated with Real Toned Irish Pipes.

FIGURE 18. Frontispiece from O'Farrell's *National Irish Music for the Union Pipes.* In the vignette, the author is depicted performing in the opera *Oscar and Malvina.*

The tenor regulator which sounds in unison with the chanter was the first regulator to be added to the pipes. A plausible explanation for the name 'union' is that this regulator and the chanter were regarded as being joined together or being in union with each other. It is quite fanciful to suggest that in the 'woollen' pipes of Shakespeare we have a misreading for *uilleann*, and on that surmise to place the origin of these pipes as far back as the sixteenth century. No explanation is offered as to how an Irish word *uilleann* could be corrupted into the English 'woollen' in sixteenth-century England, and anglicised into 'union' in eighteenth-century Ireland. However, the term *uilleann* is so widely used at present, even among pipers, that it is pedantic to object to it.

At the beginning of the present century it seemed as if the pipes were doomed to follow the harp into oblivion. In recent years, however, there has been a tremendous surge of interest, and there are now enthusiastic pipers throughout Ireland, Britain, the American continent and continental Europe. There is also an organisation, Na Píobairí Uilleann, which has for its aims the promotion of piping and the collection and preservation of music and lore about pipes and piping. Schools for piping are conducted at Belfast, Armagh, Dublin, Cork, New York, and Philadelphia, and there are makers and repairers of pipes in Derry, Belfast, Dublin, Wexford and Waterford as well as in Cork, Clare and Galway.

A full set of pipes is somewhat costly, ranging in price from £400 upwards, but as the melody in all its sweetness, it is thought by many, is best rendered on the unaccompanied chanter, one is adequately equipped with a bag, bellows and a well-fitted chanter. The other parts may be added when the player can afford them.

The war pipes are much more popular than the uilleann pipes in Ireland. There are over 250 bands in existence, and some 3,000 individual players, whose interests are catered for by two associations, the Irish Pipe Band Association, and the Scottish Pipe Band Association (Northern Ireland) Branch. Competitions for bands, solo piping, and drumming are held regularly, and members of both associations participate in these as well as in the international competitions organised by the association in Scotland.

Piping has not come down to us uninterruptedly from ancient times. There was no opportunity for martial music after the capitulation of the Jacobite army at Limerick, and the newly invented bellows pipe quickly supplanted the *píob mór* in providing music for dancing.

The traditional manner of playing on the war pipes

was lost, then, sometime during the eighteenth century. The present vogue dates back to the opening years of the present century, when members of pipers clubs in Cork and Dublin strove to re-awaken an interest in the instrument. The advance, however, particularly in recent years, when most progress was made, has been frankly on lines designed to meet the regulations for competitive playing prescribed by the Scottish piping authorities. In music, piping and drumming techniques, dress and drill, the organisation of pipe bands in Ireland may be regarded as an offshoot of the Scottish movement.

III

THE FIDDLE. Among traditional players it is believed that the pipes preceded the fiddle in Ireland as the instrument most commonly used for providing dance music, and the many references to pipes and pipers in accounts from the eighteenth century seem to confirm this view. Nevertheless, we know that the fiddle was played for dancing before the pipes emerged in their present form. Head's reference to the lasses footing it on Sundays in every field to the sound of the fiddle has already been quoted. The sound, he unkindly added, was worse than the noise made by a key upon a gridiron. An account from the end of the seventeenth century tells us that the citizens of Cork, even when they could afford nothing else, brought their children up to dance, fence, and play upon the fiddle. The instrument in question was undoubtedly the violin, which had emerged in the middle of the previous century and which is referred to invariably among traditional players as the fiddle. It is not possible to say whether earlier forms of bowed instruments were in use in Ireland immediately before its introduction, nor can we say when it was first used here to play traditional music.

The new instrument was eminently suited for the playing of dance music. It had an acceptable sound, and the fingering was flexible enough to permit all forms of ornamentation. Its use had become universal in the eighteenth century, as is evidenced by the reference to the instrument in the titles of the innumerable collections of country dances published in that century. In Scotland, it vied with the pipes as the national instrument, a host of composers of reels and strathspeys (slow reels) for the fiddle arose, and we have already mentioned Irish borrowing of some of their compositions. As these were specifically fiddle tunes, it is most likely that the instrument played a big part in popularising them here. A great deal of our own dance music was unmistakably composed by fiddle players, although the fact that relatively few tunes descend to the fourth string indicates that the pipes had a dominating influence in the creation of this music.

THE FLUTE. It is not possible to say when the flute became popular among traditional players in Ireland. The words used in Irish, *fliúit* and *fliútadóir*, to designate the instrument and the player, are obviously borrowed from English, and this suggests a late introduction. A date earlier than the eighteenth century is unlikely. The name figures in the long titles of the eighteenth century collections of country dances, in which it was usually described as the German flute, although the cylindrical bore which distinguised it from its predecessors was in all probability a French invention.

All types, from the old single-keyed to the modern fully-keyed instrument, may be observed. In some respects the older type is more suitable for playing traditional music. Sliding into the note and rolling, two favoured forms of decoration, are not possible on the modern instrument. On the open flute C natural is obtained by crossfingering, F natural by rolling the finger upwards so as to expose the hole from E through F sharp. The notes obtained in this fashion seem more pleasant than those produced by the keys.

THE WHISTLE. An ancient tale about the annual burning of Tara tells how Aileann, a chief of the Tuatha dé Danann, approached the royal residence every November eve playing fairy music which threw all the defenders into a deep sleep, leaving him free to carry out his evil work. Aileann is eventually defeated by Fionn Mac Cumhail, who has been given a special spear for the encounter and told to press the sharp edge against his forehead in order to keep himself awake when he hears the fairy music. This he does when Aileann approaches playing his sweet-stringed *Timpán* and sweet sounding *Feadán*, and so resists the sleep-inducing music. Then he pursues the fleeing Aileann and kills him at the door of his fairy residence. *Feadánaigh* or players of the *feadán*

National Museum.

FIGURE 19. Bone whistles of early 13th century found during archaeological excavation at High Street, Dublin, 1968.

are mentioned also in the ancient laws which applied to musicians who played at fairs and public sports.

What type of whistle the storyteller had in mind in this ancient saga we shall never know. We do know, however, the kind that was played centuries later in Dublin, as excavations in High Street, one of the oldest quarters of the city, have unearthed among numerous and varied objects an intact whistle belonging to the twelfth century. This is made of bone and has two finger holes. Its musical potentiality has not yet been determined (Fig. 19).

At present, two types of whistle are in use, one cone-shaped, the other cylindrical. The Clarke 'C' whistle is now the only conical or tapered whistle used by traditional players. It is made of tin, with

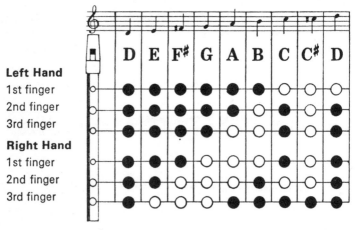

FIGURE 20. Fingering of Whistle. ● ○ denote, respectively, holes to be covered or left open. Fingering is similar for the second octave which is obtained by blowing slightly more strongly. The third finger of the right hand is replaced on the instrument as shown in order to support it while the notes A and C sharp are sounded.

an underlip of wood set into the head. Up to quite recently it was the only kind in use, bur now it has been almost superseded by the cylindrical type. It is still regarded by connoisseurs as possessing the most pleasing tone for traditional music.

The cylindrical whistle, of which the 'Generation' is the most popular kind, consists of a metal column with a plastic mouthpiece. The pitches mostly favoured are C, D, E flat, and F. In group playing, the D whistle is used, as the other instruments in the group or ensemble will be in concert pitch and the members playing in one or two sharps, as is the practice of traditional players. The small F whistle is growing in popularity as a solo instrument. It is soft and sweet sounding, and demands delicacy rather than strength in the playing.

As already mentioned, traditional players call the bottom note of the whistle 'D' irrespective of the pitch of the instrument. In this way, as is the case with the pipes and the flute, only two accidentals, C natural and F natural, will occur in the music. C natural is obtained by crossfingering; F natural is sounded by exposing the F hole in a rolling movement of the finger. The note sounded is really a long glide from E to F sharp. Theoretically, all semitones can be obtained on the whistle by forking or arching the finger so that half of the appropriate hole is uncovered. This method is not commonly adopted by traditional players, and it is scarcely practicable when playing rapid dance music.

FREE-REED INSTRUMENTS. The melodeon, concertina, accordion, and mouth organ belong to the latest family of musical instruments. Known as free-reed instruments, all appeared in one shape or another in the first half of the last century. They are sounded by a reed which consists of a strip or tongue of metal, and which is fastened over an aperture in a metal frame, through which it vibrates when air pressure is applied to it. The reeds are grouped in pairs, and air is admitted to each pair by depressing the appropriate key or button on the keyboard. A reed sounds only when the air pressure is exerted on the side from which it is fastened to the frame, and each pair of reeds is so fastened that one reed is sounded when the body or bellows of the instrument is inflated or drawn out, the other when the bellows is deflated or pressed inwards. (The mouth organ is played by blowing and suction.) In the melodeon, chromatic accordion, and mouth organ each pair of reeds is tuned to sound adjacent notes, one reed on inflation or 'on the draw', the other on deflation or 'on the press'. These instruments, on that account, are described as having single action, one movement of the instrument producing one note. The piano accordion has double action, each reed of a pair is tuned to the same pitch, and accordingly, the same note is sounded on the draw and on the press. Some concertinas have single action, others double action.

THE MELODEON. The melodeon, now described as the 'ten-keyed' melodeon to distinguish it from the later 'button' accordion, could with its single action sound twenty notes, thus giving a range of over two diatonic octaves. It was most usually pitched in 'C'. Two spoon-shaped keys on the left-hand side of the instrument provided a very simple bass, one sounding the tonic and its chord on the press, the other the dominant and its chord on the draw.

The growth in popularity of the melodeon in the closing decades of the last century coincided with the decline of the pipes throughout the country, and went hand-in-hand with the spread of the sets and half-sets, which by then had almost ousted the solo set dances.

The change in dancing was responsible, to an extent, for the changing fortunes of the instruments. The melodeon could provide the marked, uncomplicated rhythms which admirably suited the sets, and although it sounded thin and shrill, it could be heard quite clearly above all the hub-bub created by the dancers. It was much simpler to play effectively than the pipes, and the performer was not plagued as the piper still is, by struggling with ill-fitting reeds and guills. It met requirements too, at the domestic level, for the waltzes, valetas, flings, mazurkas, barn dances, and polkas which were then also in favour.

In some districts, the melodeon was often a gift from an emigrant brother or sister in Boston or New York; in others, although it cost only a few shillings, neighbours would subscribe to purchase one, and the 'joined box' would be left in a local house where there were no children. Being of sturdy construction, the 'box' (as it was usually known), needed only to be left out of the reach of children (although mice too were a hazard), and its presence on the top of the kitchen dresser or over the fireplace invited the young to try their hands at it. The melodeon, unlike the pipes or fiddle, was easy to play, and the youngest experimenter could sound musical notes. Indeed, provided with no more than a row of numbers, each one crowned with a caret, '∧', or bar, '—' on a scrap of paper, the beginner was launched at once on the way to being a box player. This system of tablature, which was in use throughout the country, indicated by the number the key to be depressed and by the sign over it whether the instrument was to be pushed in or drawn out. The melodeon also was responsible for extending music-making among the girls of the countryside, achieving a much more modest but yet more pleasurable involvement than that afforded by the piano in the cities and towns. In some districts, where fiddle and pipes were still supreme, the melodeon was referred to disparagingly as 'a woman's instrument'. Pipes and fiddles were still used almost exclusively by men, and the lady piper or fiddler was very much the exception.

CONCERTINA. The concertina, the only musical instrument invented by an Englishman, differs from the accordion in its shape: it is hexagonal. It also differs in having no bass, and in having its keyboard extended over either end of the instrument so that both hands are employed in playing the melody. Formerly, the kind mostly in use among traditional players was a cheap single-action instrument of German origin, usually having twenty keys arranged in two horizontal rows of five on either end of it. More elaborate and costlier instruments, single and double action, were, however, also available. Although its use was widespread at one time throughout the country, the concertina, was never quite as popular as the melodeon, but like the melodeon, it was a favourite among women players. Its unusual system of fingering probably saved the concertina from extinction when the accordion ousted the melodeon, but it is now almost wholly restricted to Clare and a few neighbouring areas. Signs of a revival may be detected—an inhibiting factor is the cost of a new instrument—and luckily there are still excellent players from whom traditional styles and techniques could be acquired.

THE ACCORDION. The accordion is a development of the melodeon, achieved by the addition of a second row of keys which make the instrument fully chromatic. The new or inner row is pitched a semi-tone higher than the original, and instruments are available in various pitches. Those in C/C♯, C♯/D and D/D♯ were in favour among traditional players, but they were quickly ousted by the B and C instrument, which lends itself better to the style of playing favoured by the younger players. Extra basses were also introduced, and couplers or voices were added later to provide still further effects. The use of steel instead of brass reeds was an earlier change. The overall effect of these changes was to turn a domestic instrument of somewhat wavering pitch into an instrument with a powerful tone suitable for performances in public. In so far as traditional music was involved, however, the changes were not for the better.

The accordion began to be adopted by traditional players at the end of the '20s, and in a short period almost completely replaced the melodeon. Indeed it seemed for a time as if all other instruments would fall before it. Today, however the accordion is giving way to the piano accordion and to the modest whistle.

8. Traditional Techniques and Styles

Is treise an dúchas ná an oiliúint.

AN IRISH PROVERB

I

A VIOLINIST is not an educated fiddler, any more than a fiddler is an untutored violinist. Traditional music, instrumental and vocal, is a system of music in its own right. It has its own rules, and by these it must be judged. Some of its basic rules will be set down here, and mention will also be made of other rules which do not apply to it.

(1)   (2)

FIGURE 21. The basic form of (1) the double jig and (2) the reel.

Looking at the transcription of a jig (6/8) or a reel (4/4) one sees in each bar two groups of quavers: in the jig, groups of three quavers, in the reel groups of four quavers. These little heads and tails are not arithmetical symbols. If they were, they would all have equal stress and the same length or duration. They are musical symbols which have a particular meaning for the reader, depending on the system of music in which he has been trained. Broadly speaking, the traditional musician will read these symbols in the following manner. The first accented note of the

phrase will be longest in duration and will bear the
heaviest accent. The odd beats (3rd, 5th, etc.) will
be more heavily accented then the even beats (2nd,
4th, etc.), and all will be fractionally longer than
notes without accent.

A tune is played or a song sung, not bar by bar, but
by the phrase, which very seldom is contained exactly
between bar lines. The phrase, usually the equivalent
of four bars, falls naturally into two halves, between
which there is a sense of contrast. The groups making
up these halves, the halves themselves, and the full
phrases are knitted or woven together by linking notes.
Usually this function is performed by the last note of
the group, which is thrown forward with a degree of
emphasis to the succeeding group. This forward thrust
is such a characteristic of the music that a traditional
player not familiar with musical notation will, if
asked to call the notes of a tune, invariably attach the
linking note to the group it introduces rather than to
that to which it belongs grammatically. The link
between phrases and strains may often consist of two
notes. Exceptionally, in some reels three quavers may
be used for the purpose. The reel called *The Master's
Return* affords examples of all these linkings (Fig. 22).
Intensity, the varying loudness and softness of sound,

FIGURE 22. *The Master's Return.*

is not a feature of traditional music. It is not possible, in fact, to vary the sound in such manner on the pipes. *Crescendo* and *diminuendo* are terms for which one finds no use in the notation of the music, and this rules applies equally to singing and to playing. The use of dynamics betrays the non-native.

The performer playing a tune or singing a song is not conscious of these rules, just as, when we speak, we are not conscious of the rules of punctuation or of the spelling of the words we are using. Punctuation and spelling are devices for the eye: music and speech are subjects for the ear. In fact, the two basic elements of phrasing, accent and length, can be acquired properly only by ear. There is only one way of becoming a traditional player or singer, and that is by listening to genuine material performed in a traditional manner. The general rules sketched here constitute the warp or common ground of the music, with which the local styles and techniques appropriate to the different instruments combine to form its many varied patterns. Let us look now at these two elements: the instruments in use and the local styles in which they are played.

There are two styles of playing in vogue among pipers: one called loose or open fingering, the other tight or close fingering. Formerly these different styles were regional. Thus the open fingering was found in Leinster and eastern parts of Munster, whilst tight playing was favoured in Connacht and some other districts along the western seaboard. The basic differences in the two styles result from differences in methods of fingering the chanter. In open playing, only those fingers necessary to sound the note correctly are left on the chanter; in tight playing, the only fingers taken off the chanter are those which must be taken off if the note is to sound correctly.

With the first type of fingering, one note runs into the next, producing an overall *legato* effect. Close fingering produces music which is best described as *non-legato;* there is an instant of silence between notes, since all the holes on the chanter are closed and the bottom stopped on the popping strap or little apron of leather which the piper wears above his right knee. Close fingering is the more difficult method of fingering, but it is essential for crisp, articulate piping. Regional distinctions are now lost, and players usually follow the style of the piper who most impressed them when they were learning to play.

In combination with the general features of the music, tone is the distinguishing mark of the traditional fiddler. Sweet rather than brilliant, and mellowed rather than brittle, the traditional sound is the product of the traditional manner of holding instrument and bow and of the areas of each brought into play. The forearm of the left hand, holding the neck of the fiddle, may be almost at a right angle to the body. Resting rather than held under the chin, the instrument drops at a distinct slope instead of being held at a right angle to the shoulder as is the modern habit. The wrist is not held as a swan's neck. Instead, the hand is depressed so that the neck of the instrument is supported to some extent on the ball of the hand. The bow is held somewhat rigidly above the nut, the ball of the thumb generally being flattened on the inside of the wood. The use of the bow is almost wholly restricted to the upper third, and the strings are bowed distinctly towards the end of the fingerboard, in many cases actually over it.

Only in recent years has the practice of tuning in concert pitch spread; formerly a tone, sometimes more, below was favoured. The whole effect is one of strong fingerwork with a relaxed and mellow tone rather than the hard brilliant tone favoured nowadays. People who advocate applying classical tone and technique to fiddle-playing miss the point that traditional fiddling is an art form in its own right. The techniques they seek to advance belong to a different system, and their adoption shows a pitiful ambition in the fiddler who uses them.

Although radio and gramophone have been exercising a levelling influence on traditional music, it is still possible, particularly among the older players, to distinguish different local styles. Northern players from Antrim across to Donegal favour what may be described as a single-stroke style. They produce strong vigorous music of clear tone with an economy of ornamentation. Rolling is wholly absent; the triplet played *staccato* is preferred. There are exceptions, of course, to this general description; players in Tyrone favouring embellishment. From Sligo southwards the music is much more decorated, all forms of ornamentation being used.

The whistle and flute may be taken together when talking about style. As in piping, there are two main styles. A fluid, sustained delivery is favoured in western districts, where embellishment is preferred to rhythmical ornamentation, and *staccato* playing is rarely adopted. This style of flute playing is much akin to the open style of piping. Tonguing is the characteristic feature of the second style of playing. Because the instrument lends itself more readily to it, this manner of sounding a note is used more frequently on the whistle than on the flute. Note groupings and phrases are picked out sharply, and the playing of the long notes *staccato* is a very common form of decoration. This style is not restricted to any well-defined region, but appears in areas as far apart as Cavan, Sligo, and Clare. There is little doubt that a great deal of the ornamentation used on the flute and whistle derives from piping; and this is not surprising, as most pipers can play the whistle, and many are excellent flute players.

As with the other instruments, two styles of playing on the accordion may be distinguished. The first and older style derives from the melodeon. Having only a single row of keys at his disposal the melodeon player had perforce to make frequent changes in the direction of the bellows, inwards or outwards, as the different notes required. He made a virtue of this necessity by using it to introduce rhythmic effects into his music. The phrasing was simple but the playing articulate. The single and double grace notes (described as 'splitting the note') were the more usual forms of embellishment in use. The good player, in addition, employed melodic variation. Players trained on the melodeon used the first or outer row of the accordion as they had used the single row of the older instrument, resorting only to the inner row to obtain a note not otherwise available. In this way the traditional style and technique of playing associated with the melodeon was retained almost intact.

Young players coming to the music for the first time reversed the old style altogether. They were not inhibited by any respect for tradition and quickly discovered that the easiest way to play the accordion was by using the inner row as the main one, resorting to the outer row to provide ornamentation. If the finger engaged on a key in the inner row is relaxed and slanted slightly upwards it will cover the key on the outer row sounding a semitone below, and this note is playable without having to change the direction in which the bellows is moving. Using this natural movement of the hand a whole series of triplets of the type 'cbc' can be played almost without effort. This is to use the instrument to best advantage. Unfortunately the results are too often at variance with traditional practice. The inner component of the triplet is most frequently a chromatic semitone, and with ornamentation almost wholly confined to these *legato* triplets the music seems to be extruded in one unending stream, with scarcely any articulation. The provision of the extra basses is a further source of trouble in that it permits the addition of a harmonic accompaniment which all too frequently is foreign to the nature of the music.

The introduction of the second row on the accordion effected a revolution in the style of playing, the effects of which are not confined entirely to players of the instrument, but they may be detected also in the playing of some young fiddlers. Fortunately, because of the limitations of their instruments, pipers, flute players and whistle players are largely immune from this contagion.

II

Irish folk music is essentially melodic. It uses no form of harmonic accompaniment or modulation, but relies for its effect on the ornamentation of the melodic line. Three main forms of ornamentation are employed: embellishment, variation, and rhythm. Examples of each type may be found in a single performance. Broadly speaking, however, the first or third may predominate because of the demands of the instrument being played or because it is a basic ingredient of a local style. Pipers favour a highly embellished style of playing, because this suits their instrument. Players on the concertina rely more on rhythmical or metrical variations; their instrument is not flexible enough to reproduce the grace notes employed by pipers. Northern fiddle players do not employ the form of ornamentation known as the roll; among western players it is a common form of decoration.

By embellishment is meant (a) the use of one or more grace notes, and (b) the filling in of intervals. The single grace note is very popular. It occurs usually in the form *b*A, where A, the note being decorated, is graced by a note higher in pitch. (The lower case italic indicates the grace note in each case.) The primary function of the single grace note is to emphasise an accented note, but pipers often use it to separate notes of the same pitch. It is used also to good effect before the unaccented notes of a group, imparting a lift or skip to the music. (Figs. 23 and 24, pp. 95–96.) The double grace notes in the form *ab* A are favoured by fiddle players. Melodeon players were partial to this form also. It is employed only occasionally by pipers. (Fig. 25, page 96.) In the reverse order, A*ba* much like a triplet in which the first note is rather prolonged, is a feature of fiddle playing in Tyrone and elsewhere.

The roll, or group of three grace notes, is a most effective form of decoration (Fig. 26, page 96; Fig.

(1)   (2)   (3)

FIGURE 23. Single grace notes on (1) fiddle (2) pipes and (3) accordion. Similar fingering to that given is used on the other strings of the fiddle. Gracing on the flute and whistle is similar to that on the pipes, except that the form *b*A is preferable to that of *c*A. The form *d*B is sometimes used on the pipes but the effect is somewhat coarse.

95

27, page 97.) It may be expressed as *bag*A, but the first note may be higher and the third note lower to suit the instrument played. Usually the note rolled follows a note of the same pitch, A*bag*A, but it is also used explosively, from scratch as it were. It is the essence of the roll that the middle grace note be of the shortest possible value, the slightest flick of the finger, otherwise the decoration will sound like the triplet prefixed by a grace note commonly used by box players. Rolling is not employed by fiddle players in Donegal. It fits into a fluid, flexible style of playing and would blunt the edge produced by the sharp single-bow movement favoured in that county.

(1)   (2)

FIGURE 24. Single grace notes (1) cutting or separating notes of the same pitch and (2) ornamenting unaccented notes to impart a lift or skip to the music.

(1)   (2)   (3)

FIGURE 25. Double grace notes on (1) fiddle (2) flute and whistle, and (3) accordion.

(1)   (2)

FIGURE 26. Rolls on (1) fiddle and (2) pipes, flute, and whistle. (The first roll on E in (2) is that used on the pipes.) This form of roll, known as a short roll, is used in reel playing, where it is associated with an accented crotchet, usually preceded by a quaver of the same pitch.

Groups of two, three, and four grace notes are used in piping to decorate the bottom and second notes of the chanter. In this decoration, which is known as 'cranning', it is essential that each grace note used cuts the note being cranned, that is, that no two grace notes sound consecutively. (Fig. 28 hereunder).

The second type of embellishment consists of filling in intervals, in its simplest form the interval of a third. The triplet B D B becomes BC♯DB: E G E becomes EF♯GE. This type of ornamentation reached its highest form in the elaborate *staccato* runs which the pipers of Munster introduced into their playing of laments and other slow airs. These runs no doubt represented borrowings by those pipers of harping techniques. (Fig. 29, page 98).

(1)   (2)

FIGURE 27. Further examples of rolls on (1) fiddle and (2) pipes, flute, and whistle. This form of roll, known as a long roll, is used in jigs and reels in groups comprising three quavers of the same pitch. The rhythm is like that of a free-hopping ball: the first note (or hop) is the longest, the second is longer than the third, which is somewhat shortened in time. In reels, the fourth quaver is usually thrown forward to the succeeding group.

FIGURE 28. Examples of cranning, a form of ornamentation peculiar to the pipes. The art in cranning is to ensure that no two grace notes are sounded consecutively.

97

FIGURE 29. Examples of runs, a form of ornamentation which may derive from the *sruth mór* (great stream) of the ancient harpers.

FIGURE 30. Some common forms of variation occurring in the dance music.

Variation, the second class of ornamentation, consists in changing or varying groups of notes in the course of the tune. A variation on the theme or strain itself would be regarded as an attempt at composing a new part. Two different kinds of variation occur. The simplest form consists in changing a note in a group. For example, a double jig might be regarded as starting with a triplet of quavers: the middle G could be displaced by either A, B, or D, to give GAG, GBG, or GDG. (By way of embellishment this group could be played G*agf*G Fig. 30, above.) These are the basic forms of ornamentation used by the traditional player and they come as naturally to him as a change of tone or inflexion in conversation.

The second form of variation is an entirely different matter, involving as it does a degree of instant composition. Here the group or bar is varied, perhaps only the skeleton of the phrase being retained. Each time the part is played some grouping is varied, no performance ever being the same. Two players of the past come to mind in this connexion: Michael Coleman, the Sligo fiddle player, and Johnny Doran, the piper. The ability to vary in this manner is a gift which, when combined with superior powers of execution, makes the supreme player, the virtuoso. It may be added that this is indeed a rare gift. The great majority of players who use variations of the kind in question have picked them up from other players or worked them out at their leisure. Memorised on the fingertips by practice, these variations automatically occur at the appropriate points, as do the simpler types in question above.

The third form of ornamentation, rhythmical variation, may most easily be illustrated by taking again a triplet of quavers for an example. The triplet ♫♩ may be replaced by ♩♪ (a crotchet and quaver) or by ♩ (a dotted crotchet). As already pointed out, the triplet of the jig, although comprising visually three quavers or notes of equal value, is not normally played as written. The first note is the longest; some pipers may on occasion hold it as long as the other two notes together ♩ ♫ . An effective form of variation, particularly favoured by pipers, is obtained by tapping out each note of the triplet with equal stress and length. In the group ♩ ♪ the first note might be played *staccato*, an action which gives a lift to the music. Playing the second note in that manner serves to emphasise the stress on the following accented note. The form ♩ could be rendered *staccato* as if it were a quaver followed by two quaver rests ♪ ,, or a crotchet followed by a quaver rest ♩ , . Staccato playing on the pipes and the stopping by tonguing of single notes on the flute and whistle, as in the last example, are popular forms of rhythmical variation.

Elements of these three forms of ornamentation constitute, as it were, the idioms of the music. They are present in all playing; the better the player, the greater his fluency in their use. They do not, however, exhaust the means open to him to decorate the melody. Thus double stopping, occasionally with a change in tuning, may be used by the fiddle player for greater variety. (For examples see page 133.) The piper, too, in executing a roll, particularly on the F or G in the second octave, may start the movement by gliding into the note being rolled and finish it by raising the chanter off the knee when the grace notes are being sounded. This alters the tone colour of the note and adds a touch of wildness to the melody, effects which enhance the vigour and verve present in all good reel playing.

III

Embellishment, and melodic and rhythmical variation, the main forms of ornamentation used in instrumental music, are also employed in singing. While the forms are the same, the details will vary to suit the voice, since it too is an instrument in itself. The particular form of ornamentation used will depend to an extent on the type of song being sung and also on the style of singing employed. Songs sung in a quick tempo with strong regular accent cannot be embellished in any elaborate fashion. If ornamentation is used, it will consist of slight variation of notes and rhythmical devices—stops and prolongations. A characteristic of this type of singing is the use of *one* syllable per note of music. The slower type of song permits the clustering of grace notes around a focal point of the melody and the filling in by runs of the wider intervals occurring in the air. This type or style of singing may be distinguished by the use of two or more notes to the syllable. It is a distinctively Irish style which has been adopted to some extent by the singers of songs in English.

The ornamentation here described is purely musical. Its use is not dictated by prosody or by the words of the song, although, overall, the singer fits the air to the words. The singer will avoid running out of music by accommodating excess syllables on one tone, somewhat in the manner of plain chant. On the other hand, he will provide an extra syllable to fit a spare note, making, for example, three syllables *coun-ter-ie* out of 'country' when the occasion demands it. Flexibility is the keynote of traditional singing.

Common to both styles is the use of *glissando* or sliding. A degree of nasality somewhat greater than that which is normal in speech is permitted. This feature it is which gives rise to the expression to put the 'nyea' in it, when used in relation to the singing of a traditional song. The use of vibrato, of dynamic and dramatic effects, is absolutely foreign to the traditional manner, a characteristic which is also shared with plain chant. The song will not end with a flourish. Indeed, the last few words are not uncommonly spoken in a casual throwaway manner. Time is not strictly observed; and songs with a strong accent may be *humoured* by the employment of *rubato*. In what may be regarded as older types of songs in Irish no fixed time may be employed. In transcription, such airs defy all efforts at imposing upon them any system of barring.

Quite often the traditional singer gives the impression of having pitched his voice somewhat too high. Nevertheless the voice is not forced, it is generally not much louder in volume than the normal speaking voice. The song is a communication to the company, not a speech to be delivered to the multitude. Above all, the words are the important element, the music or air being the medium for projecting or transmitting them. A song in which the words are subordinated to the music, as is often the case in concert and operatic singing, would be meaningless, traditionally. For this reason traditional singers will render every verse of a song, no matter how long it may be. It is implicit in this description of traditional singing that the solo performance is the norm. A two-part performance is unthinkable. In fact, two singing in unison is very much a contrived affair. Participation by the group or audience is exceptional, being confined, when it does occur, to the concluding line of the verse in refrain-type songs.

In concluding this short account of traditional styles and techniques a comment is required on a judgment about traditional singing which one hears with increasing frequency. *Abair amhrán* is the expression used in Irish when calling upon a person to sing. Literally, we are told, this means *say a song*. From this translation into English of the Irish phrase, it is deduced that the words and the telling of the story are the important factors in traditional singing, and, accordingly, that intensity of emotion must vary with the requirements of the words. This judgement is based solely on a mistranslation of the Irish expression, it is not supported by any observation of the material. *Abair amhrán*, if it is to be translated, means only one thing: sing a song. It does not mean *say* a song. If one wishes to have the words of a song said or spoken, the request must be framed in a different manner. The mistranslation in itself will do no harm, but the misconception based upon it could be wholly destructive of the native style of traditional singing.

9. The Great Collectors

> *It is a debt which every man owes to his country . . . to render permanent the fleeting products of every species of genius.*
> —EDWARD BUNTING in *Ancient Irish Music* (1796)

I

ALTHOUGH some Irish airs, not designated as such, had appeared in print in English collections of the seventeenth century, and some few isolated pieces even earlier still in English manuscript collections, it was not until 1726 that a collection consisting wholly of Irish music appeared. Entitled *A Collection of the Most Celebrated Irish Tunes*, and containing forty-nine airs, this work was published by John and William Neale, father and son, who carried on a music business at Christ Church Yard, Dublin. The only copy which survives, that owned by Edward Bunting, is now preserved among the collection of his manuscripts at Queen's University, Belfast. They also published *A Choice Collection of Country Dances* with their proper tunes (c. 1726) which is the earliest collection of such music published in Ireland. It is of interest to note that the Neales built the Crow Street Music Hall, in 1731, and that John was chairman of the Charitable Music Society which built the New Music Hall in Fishamble Street, where the first public performances of Handel's *Messiah* were given in 1742.

With the advance of the century, Irish airs appeared in increasing numbers in English and Scots publications, in the operas of the period, and in local collections published by the Lees and other Dublin music publishers. It was not, however, until near the close of the century that a first-hand collection of the native music appeared, that is, a collection of music taken down from performers who played it traditionally. This was Edward Bunting's *General Collection of the Ancient Irish Music*, published in 1796.

Bunting was born in the city of Armagh in 1773, the son of an Irish mother and of an English father who had come to Ireland as a mining engineer. At a very early age he displayed great musical aptitude, and when he was only eleven he was appointed substitute organist in a Belfast parish church. Bunting was first brought in contact with Irish music by his appointment as musical scribe for the Belfast Festival of Harpers which was held in July, 1792, in the Assembly Room of the Belfast Exchange. This festival was organised by some patriotic gentlemen in Belfast who hoped to preserve 'the music, poetry and oral traditions of Ireland' from extinction before the last of the old race of harpers had passed away.

Bunting, then only nineteen, was engaged 'to take down the various airs played by the different Harpers, and was particularly cautioned against adding a single note to the old melodies'. Sustained by the enthusiasm of Dr. McDonnell, who was largely responsible for organising the festival, and assisted by Arthur O'Neil and the other harpers who were present at it, Bunting began his first collection. He travelled into Tyrone and Derry, visiting Hempson, the oldest of the harpers who had attended the Belfast festival and the only one to play *ar an sean-nós* with long crooked nails. In the same year he also visited Connacht, on the invitation of Richard Kirwan, the founder of the Royal Irish Academy, who toured Mayo with him. The 1796 volume, the fruit of these labours, contains sixty-six airs, many of them published for the first time. Thomas Moore found in this first collection a veritable treasury of melody, and eight out of the twelve airs in the First Number of the *Irish Melodies* were taken by him *te bruite* out of it.

In 1802 Bunting again visited Mayo and other western counties. On this occasion he was preceded for some months by Patrick Lynch, an Irish scholar from near Downpatrick, Co. Down, whom he had employed to write down the words of the Irish songs. Unfortunately, Bunting neglected to set the airs he gathered to the Irish words recorded by Lynch. Instead, in his second volume, *A General Collection of the Ancient Music of Ireland*, published in 1809, he foolishly sought to compete with Moore by furnishing twenty airs with songs written by Thomas Campbell and other versifiers. This volume contains seventy-seven airs, but thirteen of these were repeated from the 1796 collection.

Although Bunting wrote of having made the study and preservation of Irish melodies the main business of his long life, most of the material included in *Ancient Music of Ireland*, published in 1840, had already been collected before 1809. Almost all the airs dated post 1809 by Bunting appear to have been received by him from correspondents, among whom George Petrie figures prominently. The 1840 volume was Bunting's last publication. In it he expressed the hope of re-editing and issuing his first two volumes but he did not live to accomplish this. He died in 1843 in Dublin, where he had lived for many years, and is buried there in Mount Jerome Cemetery.

Edward Bunting was the first of the great collectors of Irish folk music who notated airs from musicians in the field, in his case mostly harpers. His printed collections contain a great number of beautiful airs, many of which are known throughout the English-speaking world because of their adoption by Thomas Moore. To Bunting also we are indebted for most of our meagre knowledge of the mode and methods of playing employed by the harpers and of their lives and habits.

It would be uncritical, however, to pass on without making some reference to the manner in which Bunting treated the material he collected. In the preface to the 1840 volume he tells us that his chief aim was to guard the primitive air with religious veneration. From this one might infer that he had set down the music as he had heard it played, and that, apart from the piano accompaniments he felt obliged to provide, the tunes as published represented the original notations. This, however, was not the case. Bunting tells us that thirty was the usual number of strings found on the Irish harps at the Belfast meeting in 1792, and that the system of tuning was such that only two major scales, G and C, were perfect in their diatonic intervals. When the F strings then were tuned to F sharp, the tuning was in G major; when these strings were tuned to F natural, the tuning was in C major. In fact, in so far as tuning was involved, the harp was like a piano which had no black notes. Notwithstanding this, a great many of Bunting's airs are set in keys which the harpers could not have used; more surprisingly, his music is speckled with accidentals, for which they lacked strings.

Bunting's treatment of Carolan's well-known air *The Princess Royal* illustrates the point. He noted the tune from Arthur O'Neill, the harper, and published it in the 1840 volume (p. 35). There it appears in the key of F minor (four flats), a key in which O'Neill could not have played it. In the sixth bar (and elsewhere) Bunting makes E and D natural. Had O'Neill been able to play in the key itself, he could not have played E and D natural, since his harp had not the extra strings required for playing accidentals. It is interesting to note in the version published from Bunting's own manuscript in O'Sullivan's *Carolan* (1, p. 210) that D is not raised at all and E raised only when preceding the tonic.

In effect, what Bunting did was to alter the melody to fit what he considered to be correct and suitable harmonies. He may indeed have persuaded himself that he was correcting or improving the music. He had the curious belief that the more ancient the music, the easier it was to harmonise it, and ease of harmonisation was, he declared, a certain indication of the purity of its structure. With a show of indignation he bemoaned the fact that Moore had too often adapted the music to the words, instead of adapting the words to the music. Moore, of course, was quite within his rights in treating the music to suit his compositions. He was a writer of lyrics, not a collector of folk music. Bunting was a collector who professed to set down the airs exactly as he heard them and he had no licence to tamper with the music.

A few years after the appearance of Bunting's first volume a collection was published in London which deserves somewhat more attention than is usually given to it. This was the work of O'Farrell, a piper from Clonmel who was then settled in London. Entitled *O'Farrell's Collection of National Irish Music for the Union Pipes*, this work contains many airs and dance tunes (some of which had not previously appeared in print), as well as Scots and other non-native material. It contained also 'a Treatise with the most perfect instruction ever yet published for the Pipes'. (It is of interest to note that the volume was intended for the union pipes, not the 'uilleann' pipes.) The treatise is not really profound, but it is of value in showing that the instrument had only one regulator at this time, and for

the implication in its title that at least one other tutor
for the pipes had been published earlier.

O'Farrell's second work, his *Pocket Companion for the
Irish or Union Pipes* (c. 1810) is described in its title as
'a grand Selection of favourite Tunes, both Scotch and
Irish, adapted for the Pipes, Flute, Flageolet, and
Violin'. It contains hundreds of airs and dance tunes,
including the earliest known version of *The Fox Chase*.

The Society for the Preservation and Publication of
the Melodies of Ireland was the first organization to
concern itself with native music. It was founded in
1851, largely through the efforts of George Petrie.
Petrie, who was born in Dublin of Scots ancestry, was
a distinguished antiquary and artist, and a colleague
and friend of Eugene O'Curry and John O'Donovan,
outstanding Gaelic scholars of the day. From his boy-
hood he was interested in native music, noting down
any tune he heard which he thought unpublished
or superior to settings already in print. He conceived
it as a duty, he tells us, to preserve the native melodies,
because of a deep sense of their beauty, a strong con-
viction of their archaeological interest, and a desire to
aid in the preservation of remains so honourable to the
national character of the country. Petrie's duties as an
official of the Ordnance Survey Office gave him the
opportunity to take down airs from native musicians in
all parts of the country. His aim, however, was merely
to collect and preserve, and he had no wish to see the
results of his labour in print. Indeed, he offered his
whole collection for publication to Bunting, who de-
clined it on the grounds that should he have to acknowledge the source of this music it would be clear that the
bigger and better part was Petrie's rather than his own.

In 1851, eight years after the death of Bunting, the
Society for the Preservation and Publication of the
Melodies of Ireland was founded, and this was the

means by which a small part of Petrie's music came before the public in his own lifetime. This society, of which Petrie was president, envisaged the collection and classification of the many hundreds of unpublished airs to be found in known manuscript collections. It hoped also to establish a centre in Dublin to which persons noting down airs throughout the country might be encouraged to send them. 'The genius and expression of our music will thus be fixed and its noblest store preserved for the admiration of future ages, and the perpetual pride of the Irish race'. This impressive ideal, alas, was never realised, nor was the Society's plan for the publication annually over five years of a volume of music containing at least 200 airs, suitably arranged and containing copious notes. The Society's only collection, Petrie's *Ancient Music of Ireland*, which was published in 1855, contains only 147 airs, introduced in many cases by extensive historical and descriptive notes. A further selection of thirty-nine airs was published in 1882, sixteen years after Petrie's death. This selection is obviously incomplete, as it breaks off abruptly in the notes to the last air.

In the preface to this work, Petrie declared that Irish melodies had never been collected in any other than a careless, desultory, and often unskilful manner. These remarks were aimed directly at Bunting, with some of whose theories about the music Petrie was in total disagreement. In seeming reaction to Bunting's preference for instrumental settings, Petrie asserted that only vocal setting of airs were really trustworthy. Singers were compelled by the rhythm and metre of the words to adhere to the structure of the air; players, on the other-hand, in attempting to show their own powers of invention and execution, indulged in barbarous licence and conventionalities, and in this way often made the

airs they played almost unrecognisable. Petrie em-
phasises the point by apologising for not always being
able to obtain his own settings from the best sources; he
had to be satisfied sometimes with settings 'from pipers,
fiddlers and such corrupting and uncertain mediums'.

This is much the case of the pot calling the kettle
black. Petrie did not indeed share in the wilder fantasies
of Bunting about the nature of the music, but like him
he came to it as an outsider and brought to bear on it
notions of correct harmony which were not in fact
applicable to it.

Petrie and his eldest daughter, Maryanne, prepared
the piano arrangements for the airs in *Ancient Music of
Ireland*. To avoid grammatical errors or other glaring
defects they had submitted them for correction to a
friend who was a professor of music. The arrangements
would be regarded nowadays, however, as wholly
unsuitable, and the settings of the airs as published may
be regarded as untrustworthy, whatever their source.
Whether it was the professor, Petrie himself, or his
daughter who was responsible, the original notations
of the airs were manipulated in many instances to
meet what were then regarded as correct notions of
harmony.

A further selection from Petrie's manuscripts containing just over 200 airs was edited by Francis Hoff-
mann, and these were published with piano accompaniments, in 1877. Finally, the manuscript collection
containing a total of 2,148 pieces was entrusted by a
daughter of Petrie to Sir Charles Stanford for editing
and publication. Stanford's edition appeared in three
parts over the years 1902/5 under the title of *The
Complete Collection of Irish Music as noted by George Petrie,
L.L.D., R.H.A.*, and subsequently in a single volume.
This latter contains 1,582 tunes, Stanford having
eliminated some 500 duplicates and variants. His

editing, if such it can be called, proves he was unfitted for the task entrusted to him, since he failed to distinguish many more duplicates in the collection, or to recognise ordinary run-of-the-mill airs which were commonplace to traditional players. His system of ordering this mass of material did not extend much beyond classifying the bulk of the airs under the musically meaningless heads of those without titles, those with Irish titles, and those with English titles. The collection, therefore is a higgedly-piggedly whole with songs, dance tunes, lullabies, and marches in one unsorted mass.

Petrie had made the acquaintance of Bunting some time after the publication of the latter's second collection in 1809. When Petrie was engaged in preparing his *Ancient Music of Ireland* for the press, a young man from Glenosheen, Co. Limerick, made his acquaintance, and at his suggestion began to note down the music then current in his native county. Thus was Patrick Weston Joyce introduced to the vocation of music collecting, forming one of a trio of what may be styled the antiquarian school of Irish music, which, linking in the lives of these three collectors, extended from the late eighteenth century even into the opening decades of the present one. As Petrie had done with Bunting, so did Joyce with Petrie. He gave freely and gladly of his material to the older man. In the Stanford edition are included 195 airs which Petrie had received from Joyce, the greatest single contribution to this collection.

Joyce had hoped that the Irish Music Society would have published his collection, but the death of Petrie in 1866 put an end to that hope, since nobody else would have been capable of editing the material. Joyce then undertook the task of publishing the airs himself, and his first volume, *Ancient Irish Music,* published in 1873, contains 100 airs with pianoforte accompaniment, notes on the sources of the airs, and other interesting lore. Two ever-popular songs *Fáinne Geal an Lae* and *The Leprechaun* (with Joyce's own words) made their first appearance in print in this collection.

Two other smaller works of Joyce are worthy of mention, although not consisting of first-hand material. *Irish Music and Song*, a collection of songs in Irish which was first issued in 1887 and containing twenty songs, is the first collection of Irish songs to have the words set syllable by syllable under the appropriate notes. Another first of Joyce's is his *Irish Peasant Songs*, which contained seven songs with English words wed by him to old Irish airs. His major work, *Old Irish Folk Music and Songs*, published in 1909, contains 842 airs, and falls into three parts. The first contains material recollected by Joyce from his youth and musical transcriptions received from friends and people interested in the preservation of the music; the second contains Irish folk-songs in English, some from his own memorisings, others from broadsheets and manuscript sources. These two parts constitute roughly about half the contents. The third section is made up of transcriptions from the Forde and Pigot collections. Joyce was engaged on compiling a volume of similar composition for some years before death, which occurred in his eighty-seventh year in 1914.

On the whole, Joyce's music is much nearer the native setting than that of Bunting and Petrie. He largely avoided the fabulous keys in which the work of the two latter is almost wholly set, but his settings of dance music, like theirs, are mostly skeletal. He was, moreover, prone to altering the notation of tunes so that one cannot be certain that the published version corresponded to what he had actually heard played, or found in other sources. His treatment of the words of the songs was marred by what now would be regarded as a false respectability and literary snobbishness. The words of some songs, he tells us, were too coarse for publication or unworthy of preservation. He altered and re-edited texts and, in some cases, substituted verses composed by his brother for the words of the older songs sung by the people.

II

Rich as is the material which has been published, it is scarcely an exaggeration to say that the best collections of our native music remain unpublished.

It was mentioned in regard to Joyce's *Old Irish Folk Music and Songs* that he had included material from the Forde Collection. This collection was compiled by William Forde, a well-known Cork musician who lived in the first half of the last century. Forde was the author and editor of several musical works, and had lectured on the music of countries as far apart as China and Peru. His collection of Irish music was made between the years 1840 and 1850, chiefly in the counties of Munster, and in Leitrim and the adjacent areas of Sligo, Roscommon, Mayo, and Galway. Forde was the first collector to adapt a systematic approach in handling the material he had amassed. He procured a large manuscript volume of over 400 pages. At the top of a page he set down a tune, and under this he entered other versions of it, as well as variants and airs sharing some particular feature with it. Some 360 airs are treated in this manner; and in many cases five, six, and even more pieces are subjoined. In all, over 1,800 airs are included in the volume, from his own first-hand collecting and from printed and manuscript sources. Forde had hoped to publish this work together with a dissertation on the nature of the music and its historical importance. The prospectus dealing with the work concludes: 'Price to subscribers, one guinea. The work will go to press as soon as 250 subscribers are obtained, W. Forde, 14 Grand Parade, Cork. 1st January, 1845'. Unlike Scotland, however, Ireland lacked the nationally-minded and well-to-do patrons who might have supported such a venture, and the sum required was not forthcoming. Forde died in London five years later.

After his death his collection came into the possession of John Edward Pigot, son of the Lord Chief Baron of the Exchequer who had given Petrie some airs for his collection. (One of these, *Cathaoir an Phíobaire*, taken down from a fisherman in Kilrush in 1852, is still popular among Clare musicians.) John shared his father's interest in music, being an accomplished performer and composer. He was the author, too, of some stirring national songs which were published in *The Nation*, and was himself a collector of music. His collection contains over 3,000 items, most of which were extracted from manuscripts, chiefly of Munster origin, and from others lent to him by such well-known figures as Thomas Davis and 'Eva' of *The Nation*. He himself also collected from traditional singers and players.

Another considerable collection of folk music was compiled by Dr. Henry Hudson who was born in 1798 in the house in which Padraic Pearse was to establish St. Enda's, but which was then called 'The Fields of Odin'. This collection contains 870 tunes, of which 138 were noted from Paddy Connelly, the famous Galway piper. Others were copied from manuscripts obtained on loan and from printed volumes. Hudson was musical editor of *The Citizen*, or *Dublin Monthly Magazine*, in which he published with extensive notes selections from his own collection, as well as compositions of his own which he passed off as genuine folk-tunes. This he did in order to refute an assertion by Bunting that the last airs having any Irish character were Jackson's (the piper), and that the oldest airs were the most characteristic. Hudson's deception was successful and some of these spurious folk-airs were accepted as genuine by Petrie, Pigot, and Joyce.

Our next collector, James Goodman, really possessed the qualities essential for treating Irish music properly. He was literate musically, a native speaker of Irish, and an excellent performer on the pipes—Dubghlas de hÍde declared him to be the best piper he had ever heard. Goodman was born near Ventry in 1829, the son of the Rev. Thomas Chute Goodman, Rector of Dingle, Co. Kerry. On graduating from Trinity College, Dublin, where he had studied for the Church, he was appointed to a curacy near Skibbereen. He spent some time at Ardgroom in the Beare peninsula, and later returned to Skibbereen, where he died in 1896 at the age of sixty-seven. For the twelve years prior to his death, Canon Goodman, as he was then, was Professor of Irish in Trinity College.

Goodman compiled his collection, which is contained in four volumes, during the years 1860-66, while serving at Ardgroom. While many airs were copied from Aird, Bunting, O'Farrell, Levey, and other printed sources, the four volumes contain a wealth of dance music and slow airs noted by Goodman himself from the playing of Munster pipers. Many of the dance tunes were taken down from Thomas Kennedy, an old blind piper from Dingle who had followed Goodman to Ardgroom. Kennedy used to walk up and down the room thinking. Suddenly he would exclaim 'A Mháistir, tá ceann eile agam' (I have another one, Sir), whereupon Goodman would set it down in writing. Strangely enough, Goodman's activities as a collector of music continued only during the six years mentioned. Unfortunately, too, he appears to have been mostly concerned with instrumental music. He was wont to sing in unison with the pipes, and he exchanged the words of songs with correspondents. He made it a practice to write down the text of any song-air he notated but, unfortunately, the whereabouts of these manuscripts, if they have survived, is now unknown.

We return again to the printed collections to meet in Francis O'Neill the most colourful collector, and incomparably the greatest as far as dance music is concerned. O'Neill, who ended his career as Chief Superintendent of Police in Chicago, was born at Tralibane in West Cork in 1849. When he was sixteen, he ran away from home, reached Cork, and worked his passage to Sunderland in the north of England. He served some years before the mast, survived a shipwreck in the mid-Pacific, and landed at San Francisco, where he forsook the sea. He worked as a shepherd, a school teacher, and a railway clerk in various parts of the United States before arriving in Chicago, where he entered the police force in 1873.

O'Neill had learned to play the flute early in life, and was an accomplished player at fourteen years of age, but although he was responsible for the publication of thousands of airs and tunes he was never able, it seems, to commit music to paper. A keen ear and excellent memory, gifts shared by many traditional players, enabled him to store the melodies in his head, but it was a namesake and colleague in the police force, Sergeant James O'Neill, who committed to paper all the music which Francis had memorised from the playing of his parents and the musicians of his native district.

O'Neill, like Petrie, started his collection with a view to preserving the music and without any thought of having it published. With the accumulation of the material, however, the idea of publication grew, and the task of notation was undertaken systematically.

Tunes were noted down by James O'Neill from the playing, singing, whistling, lilting, and even the humming of contributors, played back, and corrected or accepted as the case might be. Opinions were canvassed about the contents of the proposed collection, and the consensus favoured a popular work with enough variety to satisfy every taste. A work compiled on this basis must suffer from obvious failings, and these were pointed out when *The Music of Ireland* appeared in 1903. These faults, however, do not take from the magnitude of O'Neill's achievement. His work, which was the biggest collection ever published, contained 1,850 pieces, including 625 airs, 75 tunes attributed to Carolan, 50 marches, and the stupendous total of 1,100 dance tunes.

The stature of O'Neill's achievement, never fittingly honoured in his native land, can be appreciated when we recall that Bunting's three volumes did not contain a dozen dance tunes, and the complete Petrie collection less than 300. A sidelight on the dispersal of the Irish race is shown in the fact that more than one half of the items in *The Music of Ireland* had been noted down from the singing and playing of residents in Chicago.

The *Music of Ireland* was so successful that, in response to numerous demands for a volume somewhat cheaper and containing only dance music, O'Neill produced his second collection, *The Dance Music of Ireland* (1907). This contained 1,001 dance tunes, mostly reprinted from the first volume; duplicates and some other pieces which appeared in that volume were omitted and tunes noted after its publication were included. This second volume won immediate acceptance, becoming, as it were, the bible of traditional players, so much so that when one hears the question 'Is it in the book?' the volume referred to is *The Dance Music of Ireland*. It may be mentioned that the citizens of Chicago may have unwittingly helped in the compilation of these collections since it is well known that, during O'Neill's term of office, any Irish emigrant with a good background of traditional music was assured of a place in the city police force.

O'Neill produced two other music collections: *Irish Music*, the later edition of which contained 400 pieces, and which consists of a selection made from the two volumes already published, but now with piano accompaniments; and *Waifs and Strays of Gaelic Melody*, an enlarged second edition of which appeared in 1922, which is made up of gleanings from old manuscript collections and early Scots and Irish printed sources. In *Irish Folk Music, A Fascinating Hobby* (1910), O'Neill describes his musical life and offers a fund of knowledge about Irish music and musicians based on his experiences while making his great collections.

In compiling *Irish Folk Music*, he had accumulated so much material that he decided to produce another volume in order 'to immortalise the forgotten though deserving Minstrels and Musicians of Ireland', and in the writing of this he neglected no available source of information. *Irish Minstrels and Musicians* (1913), the result of these labours, contains a vast store of information and knowledge about harpers and pipers, collectors and historians, gathered from printed sources, correspondents from all quarters of the globe, and from the many musicians then living in or passing through Chicago. A lavish collection of photographs and musical examples adds greatly to the appearance of the work. A reluctance to omit any reference, however, makes the volume somewhat diffuse, and the nostalgia and sentimentality of the exile make it somewhat syrupy in parts for home consumption. These are minor defects, however, in a pioneer work which has held the field now for over sixty years.

10. Some comments and conclusions

I

THIS short account of Irish folk music was begun by attempting to define the subject by a process of elimination. Various airs were mentioned only to be rejected, since although national and popular they were not 'the product of a musical tradition that had evolved through the process of oral transmission'. Another type of music, however, remains to be considered. Not only in Ireland, but also in Britain and the United States, reels, jigs, and hornpipes are being composed by Irish musicians, and songs are still being made in traditional moulds in Irish and in English, to commemorate stirring local or national events. Obviously these compositions cannot be described as traditional. They have not been re-shaped and re-created by the community—the process which gives the music its folk character. Must these songs and tunes too be refused admittance to the body of Irish folk music?

If a piece has been composed in a traditional form by one totally immersed in the tradition, and if it is accepted and played by traditional players as part of their repertoire, it has a claim to admittance which cannot be refused. Meeting the first condition implies that the piece conforms in content and structure to the body of native folk music; fulfilling the second condition (in which the first is implied) confirms the approval of the piece by the community. Heretofore the process of selection by the community over a lengthy period decided which pieces and forms were admitted to and retained in the national store. Nowadays, however, new compositions may be heard by more players in the course of two or three years than were the older tunes over as many generations, and an almost instant decision on the acceptance or rejection of a tune is now possible because of radio programmes and fleadhanna ceoil. Acceptance by the body of musicians in this manner is the modern equivalent of the older and more lengthy process of selection.

Except in a few cases, these modern tunes have not (as yet) appeared in print. There are, therefore, no definitive versions available by reference to which the correctness or otherwise of any setting can be determined. Traditional players are not, in any event, obsessed by the bookish idea that there can be only one correct version of a tune. The way, then, is open for reshaping in transmission and, indeed, that process can be detected already in operation on some of these new pieces.

II

It is strange that one should have to appeal to a people to become acquainted with its own music, and that folk music should have to fight for a hearing against art music. Admittedly the bias of the urban musician against folk music is not a phenomenon peculiar to Ireland, but for historical reasons the division between the performer of art music and the traditional player runs much deeper here than in many other countries. Institutes of music, whose activities centre largely on the preparation of pupils for examination, use tutors and texts which maintain a silent but effective boycott of the native music, and school authorities take something more than a musical decision in introducing the recorder and Elizabethan music into the classroom.

There is one compelling reason **why** we should know our own music: it is our own. There are reasons, too, why we should be proud of it. Enough has already been said to indicate its sheer profusion, and make us marvel at the prodigal outpouring of the spirit by what at the time was the most downtrodden and impoverished peasantry in Europe. In its variety it is startling, and it ranges from the stark archaic simplicity of its ancient marches to the riotously embellished airs that bear the words of our more lyrical love-songs. This exuberance is reflected physically in the dash and vigour of our dance music. And in form and structure, too, these airs and tunes are no less worthy of our admiration and study. In this great body of folk music we possess what should naturally be the basic musical language of the country. Students coming to a serious study of music should already have a knowledge of it. Without that knowledge, musicians in Ireland may compose music, but except in a purely geographical sense it is nonsense to hold that they can compose Irish music.

III

The best way to acquire a real knowledge of our folk music is to learn how to play it, and the easiest way to make a start is by taking up the whistle, which is the easiest instrument of all to play. All forms of ornamentation in use in rendering songs and dance music can be executed on it, and it costs only a few shillings.

There is no difficulty, therefore, in acquiring simply and at first hand a practical knowledge of this music. Its use in the classroom, moreover, offers a very easy method of introducing children to a knowledge of staff notation and the other rudiments of music.

Here it is necessary to repeat that traditional music can be learned properly only by ear, which is the way a child learns his first language. A teacher who is not himself a traditional player should go no further than demonstrating to his class the fingering for the scale. Attempting to teach airs and tunes by playing them from a printed text on the piano or other instruments, if persisted in over a period, could quite easily result in unfitting the children ever to play music in an accepted traditional style. Group playing is another modern fashion to be avoided. Certainly it is more convenient to teach an air to a group than to each individual in turn. The harm occurs in having the group reproduce the air as a group, and in training each child to subordinate or direct his activities towards achieving the desired group effect. Traditional playing, it must be remembered, is of its very nature a personal expression, and the restraint demanded in playing in a band or other ensemble kills the spirit which animates it.

If the teacher is not a traditional player the acquaintance of the pupil with the music must be developed through records and taped material, and only genuine material played in an authentic manner should be used. In this connexion it is truly a pity that radio and television programmes purporting to present traditional music cannot be unreservedly recommended. Initially, all attention should be directed to the basic rhythm of the music, as according each note in the phrase its due length and strength is the basic feature which distinguishes the traditional from the non-traditional player. Attempts at ornamentation should be deferred until some dexterity in fingering has been achieved.

When a printed text is used, as an aid to memory, in acquiring a grouping of notes which the ear refused to pick up, or later to add to one's repertoire, the text should not be regarded as sacrosanct, since a version of a tune acquires no particular validity by being committed to print. The setting played may have been good or bad; the transcription may be accurate but skeletal, defective although detailed. When the tune has been added to one's repertoire, it should be regarded as one's own. If another player has some touch or turn which appeals, there need be no hesitation about borrowing it. Imitating the style of some outstanding player is an excellent way of making progress in the initial stages of learning but it is not a course one should persist in. As soon as some proficiency has been attained, one should listen to a tune to learn it, not to acquire its style. A second-hand player always remains a second-rate player.

A comment on the transcription of tunes and on the use of such material may not be out of place. A traditional tune, we are told, evolves until it is set down in print, at which stage it becomes stereotyped or crystallised and, apparently, thereafter ceases to evolve. If this be so, it is an event which occurs wholly in academic circles. Literacy among traditional players, in Ireland at any rate, is, and always has been, much greater than many suppose, and literally thousands of pieces survive in manuscript collections written by traditional players. The ear, however, always held primacy of place and a player, while he might be acquainted with the version of a tune 'in the book', would have no high regard for a person who played it exactly in accordance with the text.

'. . . it may truly be said', writes Maurice Gorham in his *Forty Years of Irish Broadcasting*, 'that Radio Éireann, in co-operation with Comhaltas Ceoltóirí Éireann, fathered the great revival of Irish traditional music in recent years.' The regular programmes based on material collected by the Mobile Recording Unit of Radio Éireann, when introduced some twenty years ago, comprised music wholly traditional in content and style. Songs and dance music were genuine folk music, and were rendered *ar an sean-nós*, in the traditional manner. These programmes initiated a veritable new era of discovery and were avidly looked forward to by traditional musicians. Players previously unknown outside their own locality attracted listeners throughout the country; tunes scarcely known outside a parish achieved a national currency. Here indeed was a revival, or at least a reversal of the decline which had set in more than four score years previously.

It does not require any close knowledge of the situation at present to realise that this movement has not lived up to its promise, and that to speak now of a great revival of Irish traditional music is to speak of a movement which exists only in the imagination of speakers whose privilege it is to open *fleadhanna ceoil*. At their best, these radio programmes were not an unmixed blessing. The continuous broadcasting of certain tunes quickly established a popular selection, a kind of hit parade, and because of the false authority attributed to radio and print by the unsophisticated, local tunes and styles began to be abandoned. Meanwhile the decay of the genuine music continued unabated.

A radical change in the nature of these programmes occurred in recent years. Material not traditional was increasingly introduced into them, and traditional material was rendered in a manner other than traditional. This mixture of the genuine and the spurious was deliberate and was defended on the grounds that one should not make a ghetto out of Irish music. We are now informed in all seriousness that the lighter commercial ballad 'personified by the guitar as the basic accompanying instrument' must be regarded as coming within the definition of Irish traditional music.

The effect of this policy must be wholly pernicious, as the adulteration of programmes purporting to consist of traditional material confuses an ill-informed public and debases the general taste. False standards of performance are imposed upon the youth, and players and singers in possession of the genuine folk material become doubtful of its value. There can be little doubt that the survival and renewal of traditional music depend on its dissemination by radio and television, but as yet the authorities in charge of these two media have given little evidence of their awareness of the high role they could play in this field.

V

It might seem to be denying the evidence of one's senses to assert that the authentic sound of traditional music could be lost in Ireland in a very short period of time. Experience gained while engaged on compiling a complete collection of the dance music for the Department of Education convinced the author that genuine traditional players were fast disappearing and that the young people attracted to the music were acquiring, by choice, tunes made popular by public performers to the neglect of their local music and, under a misapprehension about the virtues of classical tone and techniques, were striving to play in a manner more appropriate to art than to folk music.

The position regarding traditional song was more

precarious. A field survey organised to determine whether sufficient material survived to justify collecting on a permanent basis revealed that while a wealth of material of tremendous interest had survived, the average age of the singers was over seventy years and that the impoverishing effect of pub-style singing was everywhere in evidence. One need but contemplate the fortunes of the Irish language to realise that the future of Irish traditional singing is far from rosy.

On the grounds that a good recording was the next best thing to a live performance, the Department of Education was urged to establish a national archive of traditional music. This, at length, it agreed to do but its failure to provide accommodation for the work effectively prevented its execution. On an undertaking being given by University College, Dublin, that the college would provide adequate accommodation for the archive, the work was detached from the Department and transferred to that college in 1974. In the event the move was not propitious and once more the establishment of a national archive was frustrated. Work on the completion of the dance music from which the idea of an archive had emerged has ceased and the future of this undertaking is at present uncertain.

Other organisations are involved in the promotion or presentation of traditional music. Comhaltas Ceoltóirí Éireann, the association of Irish musicians, has for its aims the promotion of the traditional music in all its forms. Its chief activity is the organisation of an annual festival of this music, Fleadh Cheoil na hÉireann, and the presentation of programmes of entertainment directed towards the tourist industry. It publishes a bi-monthly magazine, *Treoir*. A lack of discernment in distinguishing the genuine from the spurious is evident in the activities directed towards the public; the running of competitions for harp, piano or saxophone, for instance, can hardly be squared with its professed aims of promoting traditional music. Na Píobairí Uilleann, already mentioned, restricts its activities solely to piping and the pipes. Its membership confined to practitioners now exceeds 200. Its public activities embrace concerts of piping, exhibitions and lectures; its magazine, *An Píobaire*, deals with practical as well as historical aspects of the instrument and its music. Cumann Cheol Tíre Éireann, the folk music society of Ireland, in the more sober fashion of lecturing and the publication of a journal aims to encourage an informed interest in traditional music.

The music has scarcely ever enjoyed greater public acceptance since it ceased to be an integral part of the social life of the countryside than it does now in urban centres. It has attracted international attention and generated many ancillary activities. Tutors for the pipes and the whistle have appeared, general and specialist collections of dance music and song have been published; pipe makers have sprung up like mushrooms and one with difficulty keeps up with the records and tapes of the music, genuine and popular, issued by commercial recording companies. The optimist would do well to pause and reflect that the dance music has long since lost its function—providing for the needs of the dancer—and now almost wholly depends on a public most of whom are outside of its tradition. The pessimist must acknowledge that the many young players who show amazing powers of execution on pipes and fiddle, flute and whistle, will assure the continuance of the tradition into the next century. Traditional music is saved by collectors, great and small, only in the sense that butterflies are collected and saved by entomologists. Its continuity as a living thing depends on those of us who play it and upon those of us who learn it. Its future rests in our own hands.

Appendix 1

1 ÚNA BHÁN

Ó (a) Ú-na Bhán ba rós i ngair-dín
thú 's ba choinn-leoir ó-ir ar bhord na bain-rí-ona
thú, ba chláir-seach chaoin cheoil goil
romham sa mbó-thar thú. 'Sé mo léan
dó-ite nár(a) pó-sadh le do chéad searc thú.

(ii)

A Úna Bhán, nach gránna an luighe atá ort,
i do chónra chaol chláir i measc na dtáintí coirp?
Mara dtige tú le fóir orm, a phlandóig, a bhí riamh gan locht,
Ó ní thiocfaidh mé i t'áras go brách ach anocht.

(iii)

Is tá an sneachta ar a lár is tá sé dearg le fuil,
ach(a) samhail mo ghrá ní fhaca mé in áit ar bith,
tá a béal mar an siúcra, mar leamhnacht is mar fhíon ar an mbord,
Ó a chois deas lúfar a shiúlfadh gan fiar i mbróig.

(iv)

Is dhá mbeadh píopa fada cailce a'm 'gus tobac ina cheann,
óra thairneoinnse amach é agus chaithfinnse féin dhe mo sháith,
nuair d'innseoinnse dhíbhse cé gcónaíonn Úna Bhán
Ó i gCill Bhríde atá sí sínte is tá leac ar a ceann.

2 SÉ OAKUM A' PHRÍOSÚIN

O 'gus mol- aim sú na heor-nan go deo a- gus choí-chin. Nach
Is for- aim de dy-dil- ó- rum, sé oa- kum a' phrío-súin, is gur

mair-g nach (a) mbíonn tóir ag (e) Rí Seoir- se ar adhéa-namh? Seán
fhá-ga sú na   heor-nan   na hó- glaigh dhá spío-nadh

Forde a bheith 'na ghiúis-tís, sé chomhair-leodh na daoi- ne,   mar

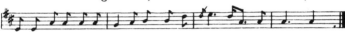

b'eis-ean a chuir ar an eo- las dhom- sa le oa- kum a spío- nadh.

(ii)

'gus maidin ins an tSamhradh is mo leaba déanta síos a'm,
d'éirigh mé mo sheasamh nó gur bhreathnaigh mé mo thimpeall,
sea chuala mé an *hello* orm is cén deabhail atá tú a dhéanamh,
do dhá láimh in do phócaí 'gus oakum le spíonadh?
    Is foram, etc.

(iii)

Is chuaigh mé féin i stór is bhí oakum thar maol ann,
thug mé lán mo ghabhlach liom, mo dhóthain go ceann míosa.
Is nach mise a bhain an gáire as an ngarda a bhí mo thimpeall,
nuair d'fhiaraigh mé den cheannphort arb air a d'fhás an
    fionnach?
    Is foram, etc.

(iv)

Is nach mise a bhíonns go brónach gach Domhnach is lá saoire,
mo sheasamh amuigh san ngairdín istigh i bhfáinne's mé goil
    timpeall?
Is gur sileann ó mo shúile sruth deora nuair smaoiním
gurb olc an obair Domhnaigh bheith i gcónaí ar an gcaoi seo.
    Is foram, etc.

129

3 LORD BAKER

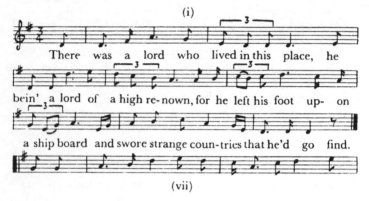

(i)

There was a lord who lived in this place, he
bein' a lord of a high re-nown, for he left his foot up-on
a ship board and swore strange coun-tries that he'd go find.

(vii)

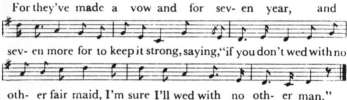

For they've made a vow and for sev- en year, and
sev- en more for to keep it strong, saying,"if you don't wed with no
oth- er fair maid, I'm sure I'll wed with no oth- er man."

(ii)

For he travelled east and he travelled west
(And half the south and the east also)
Until he 'rived into Turkey land
There he was taken and bound in prison
Until his life it was quite wearee.

(iii)

Oh a Turkey bold had one only daughter,
As fair a lady as your eyes could see,
For she stole the keys of her dado's harbour
And swore Lord Baker that she'd set free.

(iv)

Saying, 'you have houses and you have living
And all Northumber belongs to thee,
What would you give to that fair young lady?
It is out of trouble would set you free?

Saying, 'I have houses and I have living
And all Northumber belongs to me,
I would will them all to that fair young lady
It is out of trouble would set me free'.

For she brought him down to her dado's harbour
And filled for him was the ship of fame.
And at every toast that she did drink round him,
'I wish Lord Baker that you were mine'.

Oh seven year it was past and over
And seven more it was rolling on,
When she bundled up all her gold and clothing
And swore Lord Baker that she'd go find.

For she travelled east and she travelled west
Until she came to the palace of him,
'Who is that, who's that,' replies the porter,
'that knocks so gently and can't get in?'

'Is this Lord Baker's palace,' replies the lady,
'or is his lordship himself within?'
'This is Lord Baker's palace,' replies the porter,
'But this very day took a new bride in'.

'Will you tell him send me a cut of his wedding cake,
And a glass of his wine, it being ere so strong,
and to remember that fair young lady
Who did release him in Turkey land?

In goes, in goes, was the young bold porter
And kneel down gently on his right knee.
'Rise up, rise up, it's my young bold porter,
What news, what news have you got for me?'

. . . . . .

Saying, 'I have news of a greatest person
As fair a lady as my eyes could see
She's at the gate waiting for your charitee.'

(xiv)

She's wears a gold ring on every finger
And on the middle one where she wears three
And she has more gold hung around her middle
Then'd buy Lord Thumber and fambily.

(xv)

She told you send her a cut of your wedding cake
And a glass of your wine, ere being ere so strong
And to remember that fair young lady
Who did release you in Turkey land.'

(xvi)

For he caught the soowerd (:sword) just by the middle
And he cut the wedding cake in pieces three,
Down comes, down comes, was the young bride's mother,
'Oh what will I do for my daughter dear?'

(xvii)

'I owned your daughter is none discover, (?)
And none the better is she to me.
Your daughter came with one pack of gold
I'll revert her home, love, with thirty-three.'

Úna Bhán and *Sé Oakum a' Phríosúin* were sung by Seán ac Donncha (Carna, now living at Áth Eascragh Co. Galway) and recorded in Avondale Studio, Dublin. For another version of *Úna Bhán* see *Deora Aille* (referred to at page 143 hereunder). Further texts may be found in *Ceol na n-Oileán* by An tAthair Tomás Ó Ceallaigh. *Lord Baker* was recorded in 1967 by Tom Munnelly (Dublin) from the singing of John Reilly who was then living at Boyle, Co. Roscommon, where he died in May, 1969. The varying of the melody to which the different verses of a song are sung, a characteristic of Reilly's singing, is not a usual feature among traditional singers in Ireland. For an account of this ballad and other texts see Child's *The English and Scottish Popular Ballads* (no. 53).

The music was transcribed by Pádraig Ó Máille, the texts by Breandán Breathnach.

4 THE CONGRESS REEL

5 THE FOXHUNTER'S REEL

6 WITHIN A MILE OF DUBLIN

7 THE GANDER IN THE PRATIE HOLE

8 THE TRIP TO KILLAVEL

9 HARDIMAN THE FIDDLER

10 THE HUMOURS OF WHISKEY

11 THE WHINNY HILLS OF LEITRIM

12 GUSTY FROLICS

13 ELIZABETH KELLY'S DELIGHT

14   MARY BRENNAN'S FAVOURITE

15   THE HUMOURS OF KILCLOGHER

16   ASK MY FATHER

17 PATSY MACK

18 MY LOVE IN THE MORNING

19 AN CHEARC AR FAD IS AN ANAIRTHE

20 TOMEEN O'DEA'S REEL

21 IS TRUA GAN PEATA AN MHAOIR AGAM

22 THE BALLYKETT COURTHOUSE

23 THE HUMOURS OF TUAIMGREINE

24 McDERMOTT'S HORNPIPE

D.S.

25 DUNPHY'S HORNPIPE

26 CONCERTINA HORNPIPE

27 THE EBB TIDE

28 THE HUNT

29 AN SÚISÍN BÁN

30 FRAHER'S JIG

Performers: Seán Keane fiddle nos 4, 5, 7 and 8: Pat Mitchell pipes nos 6, 16, 25 and 30: Michael Tubridy flute nos 9, 10, 11, 28 and 29: whistle nos 17, 18, 19, 20, 21 and 22: Paddy O'Brien accordion nos 12, 23 and 24: John Kelly fiddle nos 13, 14 and 15: concertina nos 26 and 27. The first and second strings of the fiddle were tuned a tone down in playing nos 4 and 5. Musical transcriptions by Breandán Breathnach.

Appendix 11

Selected Recordings of Irish Traditional Music and Song

Adam in Paradise. Eddie Butcher. Songs in English. Transcription of texts and editorial notes by Hugh Shields.
45 r.p.m., UFM 1, Ulster Folk Museum, Co. Down.

Deora Aille. Máire Áine Ní Dhonnchú. Songs in Irish. Transcription of texts and translation by Seán Mac Mathúna.
Claddagh Records, Dublin.

Grand Airs of Connemara and *More Grand Airs of Connemara*. Páraic Ó Catháin, Seán Mac Donnchú and Páraic Ó Neachtain. Songs in Irish. Festy Ó Conluain. Airs on whistle. Transcription and translation of texts by Breandán Breathnach.
L.P. 12 T 177 and L.P. 12 T 202, Topic Records, London.

Joe Heaney. Songs in Irish and English.
L.P. 12 T 91, Topic Records, London.

Minstrel from Clare, The. Willie Clancy. Dance music and airs on pipes and whistle with songs in English.
L.P. 12 T 175, Topic Records, London.

Rí na bPíobairí. Leo Rowsome. Dance music and airs on pipes.
L.P. CC 1, Claddagh Records, Dublin.

Star above the Garter, The. Denis Murphy and Julia Clifford. Dance music and airs (together and solo).
L.P. CC 5, Claddagh Records, Dublin.

Music from Sliabh Luachra.
L.P. 12 T 309-11, Topic Records, London.

John Kelly. Fiddle and concertina player.
L.P. 12 TFRS 504, Topic Records.

The Flowing Tide. Chris Droney.
L.P. 12 TFRS 503, Topic Records.

Uilleann Pipes. Pat Mitchell.
L.P. 12 TS 294, Topic Records.

The last of the Travelling Pipers. Felix Doran
L.P. 12 T 288, Topic Records.

The Legacy of Michael Coleman.
L.P. 33002, Shanachie.

The Wheels of the World.
L.P. 45001, Morning Star Records.

Forty years of Irish piping. Séamus Ennis.
L.P. Green Linnet Innisfree Records, Conn., U.S.A.

The Drones and the Chanters. Irish Pipering.
L.P. CC 11, Claddagh Records, Dublin.

Appendix III

Glossary of Irish Words and Translations

p 1 Bím lá binn agus lá searbh: I am sweet by times and sour
by times.
amhráin atá i mbéal an phobail: songs in the mouth of the
public, songs that are popular.

p 2 Gaeltacht: districts in which Irish is vernacular.
Galltacht: districts in which English is vernacular.
suantraí: slumber music
geantraí: laughter music
goltraí: crying music
Magh Tuireadh: Moytura, Co. Sligo.

p 4 suantairghléas: slumber inducing instrument.
geantairghléas: laughter inducing instrument.
goltairghléas: crying inducing instrument.

p 20 reacaire: reciter.

p 22 (1) She is more beautiful than the autumn sun,
and after her honey forms
in the track of her feet in the mountain,
however cold the weather after November.

(2) How delightful for the booth in which my love
goes drinking,
how delightful for the path on which he lays a foot
how delightful for the young maiden who gets
him in marriage,
Guiding star of the morning and lighted torch
of the evening.

(3) and sweeter is the taste of her kiss
than the sugar of bees on table
and its being drunk through blood-red brandy.

p 23 Druimíonn/Droimeann: a white-backed cow

p 24 laoithe: lays
Fianaíocht: the branch of literature dealing with Finn and
his companions.

p 26 Finn had Sceolán and Bran
ready on a leash in his fist,

Each member of the Fian had his hound
and our sweetmouthed hunting dogs making music.

p 26 laoi: a lay

p 28 The old women of the district would give me
  neither wife nor dowry
 And I promised the maiden I should for ever follow her.

p 37 It is a pity I have not the steward's pet,
 It is a pity I have not the steward's pet,
 It is a pity I have not the steward's pet,
 and the little white sheep
  And oh, bravo, bravo,
 Love of my heart, without deciet.
  And oh, bravo, bravo,
  You are your mother's little pet.

p 38 Raingce timcheall teinte: Dance around fires

p 42 Maide na bplanndaí: the planting stick, dibbler
 rince an chipín: the little stick dance
 step an chipín: the little stick step
 Tá dhá ghabhairín buí agam: I have two little goats

p 43 Damhsa na gCoinín: the rabbit dance

p 48 rincí Gaelacha: Irish dances

p 54 go ndéana Dia grásta orthu ar fad: may God grant
  them all grace.

p 63 portaireacht: mouth music
 poirt bhéil: mouth tunes

p 88 Is treise etc; nature is stronger than training

p104 ar an sean-nós: in the old way, traditional

p105 te bruite: directly, immediately, hot boiled

p124 fleadhanna ceoil: music festivals

p128 Fair Una (Oonagh)

(i)

O, fair Una, you were a rose in a garden,
A golden candle-holder on the queen's table,
A sweet musical harp preceding me on my road,
My great misfortune that you were not married
 to your first love.

(ii)

Fair Una, how hateful is your situation,
 in your narrow coffin of boards in the midst
  of the hosts of the dead,
If you do not come to succour me, O stripling
  ever faultless,
I shall never again after tonight enter your abode.

The snow has fallen and it is red with blood,
the like of my love I never saw anywhere,
her mouth is as sugar, as new milk, and as wine
    on the table,
O, pretty nimble foot which would walk without
    going awry in shoes.

Had I a long clay pipe with tobacco in its head
O, I should draw it out and smoke of it my fill,
when I should tell you were fair Una dwells,
In Kilbride she is laid and a tombstone above
    her head.

The Prison Oakum

O, I praise the barley juice for ever and always,
What a pity King George does not wish to make it.
John Forde as justice he would advise the people,
for 'twas he put me in the way of knowing how to
    pick oakum.
and forum de dydilorum, 'tis the prison oakum
and the juice of the barley left the volunteers picking it.

One Summer's morning with my bed made up
    I stood up to look around,
then I heard the 'hello' directed towards me
    and 'what the devil are you doing?'
your two hands in your pockets and oakum to be picked'.
    and forum etc.

And I entered a store overflowing with oakum,
took the full of my arms, enough to do me a month,
Wasn't it I knocked a laugh out of the guards who
    were around me,
When I asked the superintendent was it on himself
    the hair grew.
and forum etc.

Is it not I who is sorrowful on Sundays and holidays
Standing out in the garden, going around inside a ring
and a stream of tears flow from my eyes when I remember
that it is poor work on Sundays forever to be so.
and forum etc.

Bibliography

Only books which are in print or which may be obtained through a library are included. Works marked with an asterisk contain music.

Breathnach, Breandán. *Ceol Rince na hÉireann. Dublin, 1963. *Ceol Rince na hÉireann II. Dublin 1976.

Bunting, Edward. *Ancient Irish Music (1796) *Ancient Irish Music (1809) *Ancient Music of Ireland (1840). Republished in one volume, Dublin, 1969.

*Ceol. A Journal of Irish Music. (vol. 4 No. 3 In Progress). Dublin.

Collinson, Francis. *The Traditional and National Music of Scotland. London, 1966.

De Noraidh, Liam. *Ceol ón Mumhain. Dublin 1965.

*Éigse Cheol Tíre/Irish Folk Music Studies. (vol. 2 in progress). Dublin.

Joyce, P. W. *Ancient Music of Ireland. Dublin, 1912.

Mac Coluim, Fionán. *Cosa Buidhe Arda. Dublin, 1924. *Amhráin na nGleann. Dublin 1939.

Mitchell, Pat. *The Dance Music of Willie Clancy. Cork 1976.

Ní Annagáin, M. agus De Chlanndiolúin, S. *Londubh an Chairn. London, 1927.

Ó Baoighill, Seán. *Cnuasacht de Cheoltaí Uladh. Belfast, 1944.

O'Boyle, Seán. *The Irish Song Tradition. Dublin, 1976.

Ó Ceallaigh, An tAthair Tomás. Ceol na nOileán. Dublin, 1931.

Ó Duibhginn, Seosamh. *Dónall Óg. Dublin, 1960.

O'Keefe, J. C. and O'Brien, Art. A Hand Book of Irish Dances. Dublin, 1954.

Ó Lochlainn, Colm. *Irish Street Ballads. Dublin, 1939. *More Irish Street Ballads. Dublin 1965.

Ó Máille, Mícheál agus Tomás. Amhráin Chlainne Gaedhal. Dublin, 1925.

Ó Muirgheasa, Énrí. Céad de Cheoltaibh Uladh. Dublin, 1915. *Dhá Chéad de Cheoltaibh Uladh. Dublin 1969.

O'Neill, Francis. *The Music of Ireland*. New York, 1964. *The Dance Music of Ireland*. Dublin, 1969. *Irish Folk Music; A fascinating study*. Chicago, 1910. *Irish Minstrels and Musicians*. Chicago, 1913. *Waifs and Strays of Gaelic Melody*. Chicago, 1922.

O'Sullivan, Donal. *The Bunting Collection of Irish Music and Songs* in *Journal of the Irish Folk Song Society*, (Reprint) vols. v and vi. *Songs of the Irish*. Dublin, 1967.

Ó Tuama, Seán. *An Grá in Amhráin na nDaoine*. Dublin, 1960.

Ó Tuama, Seán Óg. *An Chóisir Cheoil i-xii*. Dublin.

Petrie, George. *Ancient Music of Ireland*. Farnborough, 1968.

Rimmer, Joan. *The Irish Harp*. Dublin, 1977.

Roche, F. *Irish Airs, Marches and Dance Tunes I-III*. Dublin, I and II 1911, III 1927.

Stanford, C. V. *The Complete Collection of Irish Music as noted by George Petrie, LL.D., R.H.A. (1789-1866)*. London, 1902-1905.

Vallely, B. *Learn to play the Uilleann Pipes*. Belfast, 1976.

Vallely, E. *Learn to play the tin-whistle I-III*. Belfast, 1973. *Sing a Song I-III*. Belfast, 1976.

Zimmermann, G. *Songs of Irish Rebellion*. Dublin, 1967.